Laboratory Manual

CONCEPTS AND CHALLENGES

LIFE ◆ SCIENCE

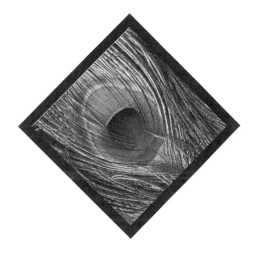

Martin Schachter ◆ Alan Winkler ◆ Stanley Wolfe

Stanley Wolfe
Project Coordinator

GLOBE FEARON
Pearson Learning Group

The following people have contributed to the development of this product:

Art and Design: Evelyn Bauer, Susan Brorein, Tracey Gerber,
Bernadette Hruby, Carol Marie Kiernan, Mindy Klarman, Judy Mahoney,
Karen Mancinelli, Elbaliz Mendez, April Okano, Dan Thomas, Jennifer Visco

Editorial: Stephanie P. Cahill, Gina Dalessio, Nija Dixon, Martha Feehan,
Theresa McCarthy, Maurice Sabean, Marilyn Sarch, Maury Solomon,
S. Adrienn Vegh-Soti, Shirley C. White, Jeffrey Wickersty

Manufacturing: Mark Cirillo, Tom Dunne

Marketing: Douglas Falk, Stephanie Schuler

Production: Irene Belinsky, Linda Bierniak, Carlos Blas, Karen Edmonds,
Cheryl Golding, Leslie Greenberg, Roxanne Knoll, Susan Levine, Cynthia Lynch,
Jennifer Murphy, Lisa Svoronos, Susan Tamm

Publishing Operations: Carolyn Coyle, Thomas Daning, Richetta Lobban

Technology: Ellen Strain

About the Cover: Life science is the study of living organisms and their life processes.
The images on the cover represent many of the subjects that you will be learning about
in this book. The polar bears' white fur and thick insulation are adaptations that have
evolved over time to help them survive in a harsh environment. Among the six
characteristics of living things is the ability of organisms to produce more organisms of
their own kind. In addition to the parent-child relationship shown here, polar bears
interact with other species. The inset photograph is of a peacock's feathers. The male
peacock uses his colorful feathers to attract a mate during a courting ritual. What do
you think are some other things that you will study in life science?

1-800-321-3106
www.pearsonlearning.com

CONTENTS

SAFETY IN THE SCIENCE LABORATORY

Unlike many other fields of study, science allows you an opportunity to "learn by doing." Part of this process often involves work both in the laboratory and in the field.

Working a science laboratory can be both exciting and meaningful. However, when carrying out experiments, you may sometimes work with materials that can be dangerous if not handled properly. For this reason, you must always be aware of proper safety procedures. You can avoid accidents in the laboratory by following a few simple guidelines:

- **Always** handle all material carefully.
- **Never** perform a laboratory investigation without direction from your teacher.
- **Never** work alone in the science laboratory.
- **Always** read directions in a laboratory investigation before beginning the laboratory.

Throughout this laboratory program, you will see the safety symbols that are shown below and on the next page. Before beginning any laboratory, be sure to read the laboratory and note any safety symbols and caution statements. If you know what each symbol means, and always follow the guidelines that apply to each symbol, your work in the laboratory will be both safe and exciting.

SAFETY SYMBOLS

 Clothing Protection
- Wear your laboratory apron to protect your clothing from stains or burns.

 Eye Safety
- Wear your laboratory goggles, especially when working with open flames and chemicals.
- If chemicals get into your eyes, flush your eyes with plenty of water. Notify your teacher immediately.
- Be sure you know how to use the emergency eyewash system in the laboratory.

 Clean Up
- Always wash your hands after an activity in which you handle chemicals, animals, or plants.

 Disposal
- Keep your work area clean at all times.
- Dispose of all materials properly. Follow your teacher's instructions for disposal.

 Glassware Safety
- Handle glassware carefully.
- Check all glassware for chips or cracks before using it. Never use glassware that has chips or cracks.
- Do not try to clean up broken glassware. Notify your teacher if you break a piece of glassware.
- Air-dry all glassware. Do not use paper towels to dry glassware.
- Never force glass tubing into the hole of a rubber stopper.

 Heating Safety
- Be careful when handling hot objects.
- Turn off the hot plate or other heat source when you are not using it.
- When you heat chemicals in a test tube, always point the test tube away from people.

Fire Safety
- Confine loose clothing and tie back long hair when working near an open flame.
- Be sure you know the location of fire extinguishers and fire blankets in the laboratory.
- Never reach across an open flame.

 Dangerous Chemicals
- Use extreme care when working with acids and bases. Both acids and bases can cause burns. If you spill an acid or a base on your skin, flush your skin with plenty of water. Notify your teacher immediately.
- Never mix chemicals unless you are instructed to do so by your teacher.
- Never pour water into an acid or a base. Always pour an acid or a base into water.
- Never smell anything directly.
- Use caution when handling chemicals that produce fumes.

 Poison
- Never use chemicals without directions from your teacher.
- Use all poisonous chemicals with extreme caution.
- Inform your teacher immediately if you spill chemicals or get any chemicals in your eyes or on your skin.

 Sharp Objects
- Be careful when using scissors, scalpels, knives, or other cutting instruments.
- Always dissect specimens in a dissecting pan. Never dissect a specimen while holding it in your hand.
- Always cut in the direction away from your body.

 Electrical Safety
- Check all electrical equipment for loose plugs or worn cords before using it.
- Be sure that electrical cords are not placed where people can trip over them.
- Do not use electrical equipment with wet hands or near water.
- Never overload an electrical circuit.

 Plant Safety
- Never eat any part of a plant that you cannot identify as edible.
- Some plants, such as poison ivy, are harmful if they are touched or eaten. Use caution when handling or collecting plants. Always use a reliable field guide to plants.

 Animal Safety
- Be careful when handling live animals. Some animals can injure you or spread disease.
- Do not bring live animals into class that have not been purchased from a reputable pet store.

 Caution
- Follow the △ CAUTION and safety symbols you see used throughout this manual when doing labs or other activities.

LIFE SCIENCE EQUIPMENT AND APPARATUS

As you work in the life science laboratory, you will need to become familiar with many pieces of equipment and apparatus. Several common pieces of equipment are shown below and on the next page. Below the name of each piece of equipment is a brief description of what the equipment is used for.

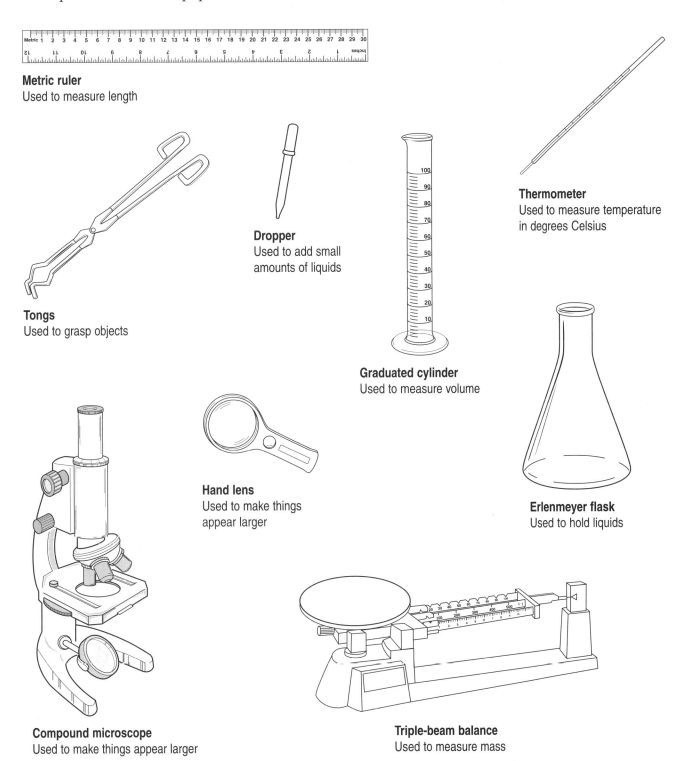

Metric ruler
Used to measure length

Tongs
Used to grasp objects

Dropper
Used to add small amounts of liquids

Graduated cylinder
Used to measure volume

Thermometer
Used to measure temperature in degrees Celsius

Erlenmeyer flask
Used to hold liquids

Hand lens
Used to make things appear larger

Compound microscope
Used to make things appear larger

Triple-beam balance
Used to measure mass

LIFE SCIENCE EQUIPMENT AND APPARATUS

Funnel and filter paper
Used to separate mixtures

Microscope slides and coverslips
Used for viewing and protecting
specimens under a microscope

Petri dish and lid
Used to hold materials,
such as bacteria

Beakers
Used to hold materials

Hot plate
Used to heat materials

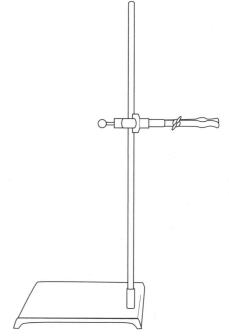

Ring stand with clamp
Used to hold equipment steady

Test tube holder
Used to hold hot
test tubes

Plastic pipette
Used to extract or dispense
small amounts of liquids

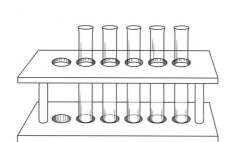

Test tubes and rack
Used to hold materials

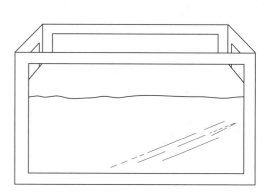

Aquarium
Used to hold large amounts of
water and aquatic organisms

LABORATORY SKILLS WORKSHEET 1

Using a Graduated Cylinder

BACKGROUND: A graduated cylinder is used to measure the volume of a liquid. A graduated cylinder is a long tube marked along its side with lines that show the volume. Some graduated cylinders are small and measure only up to 10 milliliters of liquid. Others are larger and measure 25 milliliters, 100 milliliters, or more. Notice the 10-milliliter graduated cylinder in Figure 1. The long lines below the numbers show milliliters. The shorter lines show two-tenths of a milliliter. Other graduated cylinders may have different values for the long and short lines. When you pour a liquid into a graduated cylinder, you can use these lines to determine the volume of the liquid.

PURPOSE: In this activity, you will learn how to use a graduated cylinder.

PROCEDURE

Part A: Reading a Graduated Cylinder

☐ 1. **OBSERVE:** Look at a graduated cylinder. Notice the markings on the side. The markings on a graduated cylinder are usually given in milliliters, which is abbreviated mL. Record information about this graduated cylinder in Table 1 on page 6.

☐ 2. Look at the graduated cylinder shown in Figure 2. Notice that the surface of the liquid is curved upward at the sides. This curve is called a meniscus. When you read the volume of a liquid in a graduated cylinder, you must look at it from eye level. Always read the volume at the flat, center part of the meniscus. In Figure 2, the volume is 8.6 mL.

☐ 3. Look at the graduated cylinder readings in Figure 3. Write the volume of the liquid in each graduated cylinder in the space provided.

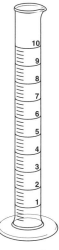

▲ **Figure 1** A 10-mL graduated cylinder

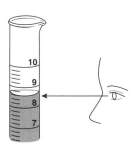

▲ **Figure 2** Reading the meniscus of a liquid in a graduated cylinder

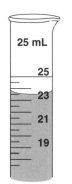

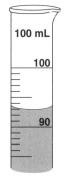

1. _____ 2. _____ 3. _____ 4. _____

▲ **Figure 3** Write the volume of liquid in each graduated cylinder.

Part B: Measuring the Volume of a Liquid

❏ 1. **MEASURE:** Half fill a small jar with water. Pour the water into the graduated cylinder. Record the volume of the water in Table 2. Ask your teacher to check your answer. Empty your graduated cylinder.

❏ 2. Repeat Step 4 two more times. Have your lab partner check your answers.

❏ 3. **MEASURE:** Use a graduated cylinder to measure 64 mL of water. First, fill the jar with water. Pour water from the jar into the graduated cylinder until it is between the 60 and 70-mL mark. Look at the meniscus from eye level. If the reading is greater than 64 mL, pour some of the water back into the jar. If the reading is less than 64 mL, use a dropper to get water from the jar and add it to the graduated cylinder. Continue until the lower part of the meniscus is on the 64-mL line.

❏ 4. Repeat Step 3 to measure 82 mL and 93 mL. Have your lab partner check your readings each time.

OBSERVATIONS

Table 1: Information About the Graduated Cylinder	
Greatest volume it will measure	
Volume shown by the longest lines	
Volume shown by the shortest lines	

Table 2: Reading a Graduated Cylinder	
Volume 1	
Volume 2	
Volume 3	

CONCLUSIONS

1. **COMPARE:** What is an advantage of measuring a liquid with a graduated cylinder instead of a beaker? _____

_____

2. **INFER:** If the smallest markings on a graduated cylinder are 1 mL apart, is it possible to measure a volume of 63.5 mL? Explain your answer.

_____

_____

3. Suppose that the long markings on a graduated cylinder are 1 mL apart and there are four short lines between the 8-mL and the 9-mL marks. What volumes do the short lines indicate?

_____

_____

LABORATORY SKILLS WORKSHEET 2

Using a Triple-Beam Balance

Materials

solid object

beaker

salt

tablespoon

triple-beam balance

BACKGROUND: Triple-beam balances are often used to find the mass of solid objects or powdered solids. Most triple-beam balances have a balance pan, three beams, a pointer, and a three-part scale with riders. Many balances also have an adjustment knob. The scale of a balance measures grams. The scale of the top beam gives readings in 10-gram intervals, for example, 10 grams, 20 grams, and so on, up to 100 grams. The scale of the middle beam gives readings in hundreds of grams. The scale of the bottom beam gives readings in grams from 1 gram to 10 grams. Each 1-gram interval shows tenths of a gram, from 0.1 gram to 0.9 gram. A triple-beam balance measures the mass of an object by balancing the mass in the pan with the riders on the scale.

PURPOSE: In this activity, you will learn how to use a triple-beam balance.

PROCEDURE

Part A: Reading a Mass

❏ **1.** To read the mass of an object, read the position of the hundreds, tens, and ones riders to find the mass in hundreds, tens, ones, and tenths of grams. Read the mass shown on the triple-beam balance scale below.

❏ **2.** **RECORD:** Record the mass shown by each rider in Table 1. Make sure that you write a decimal point before the number of tenths shown on the ones rider.

Table 1: Reading a Mass	
Rider	Mass
Tens rider	
Hundreds rider	
Ones rider	
Total mass	

❏ **3.** Add the masses together to find the total mass. Record this in Table 1.

Part B: Finding the Mass of a Solid Object

❏ **1.** Before using a triple-beam balance, make sure that the balance is centered properly. Set all the riders to zero. The balance pointer should rest at the zero mark at the end of the scale. If the balance pointer is not at zero, turn the adjustment knob until the pointer arrives at zero.

❏ 2. Place the object on the balance pan.

❏ 3. **MEASURE:** Slide the riders until the pointer is once again on zero. This means that the scale is balanced. If the mass of the object is less than 10 grams, you will find that you do not need to move the top rider. If the mass of the object is less than 100 grams, you will not need to move the middle rider.

❏ 4. **RECORD:** To find the mass of the object, first record the measurement shown on each of the three riders. Record this information in Table 2. Then, add the masses of each rider to find the total mass. Record your measurement in Table 2.

Part C: Finding the Mass of a Substance

❏ 1. **MODEL:** Place a beaker on the balance pan to find its mass. Record this mass in Table 3.

❏ 2. **MEASURE:** Place 1 tablespoon of salt in the beaker. Find the mass of the beaker and the salt combined. Record the mass in Table 3.

❏ 3. **CALCULATE:** To find the mass of the salt alone, subtract the mass of the beaker from the combined mass of the beaker and salt. Record the mass of the salt in Table 3.

OBSERVATIONS

Table 2: Reading a Mass	
Rider	**Mass**
Tens rider	
Hundreds rider	
Ones rider	
Total mass	

Table 3: Finding the Mass of a Substance	
Mass of beaker (a)	
Mass of beaker plus salt (b)	
Total mass (b minus a)	

CONCLUSIONS

1. **CALCULATE:** What is the greatest mass that most triple-beam balances can accurately

   measure? _____

2. **INFER:** If only the ones rider needs to be moved from zero to balance a mass on the

   the balance pan, what is the largest mass that the object can have? _____

3. **INFER:** If the hundreds rider is left at zero and the tens and ones riders are moved to
   balance the scale, what is the largest mass that the object in the balance pan can have?

   _____

Name _____ Class _____ Date _____

Measuring Volume and Density

BACKGROUND: When you blow up a balloon, you force air into the balloon. The volume of the balloon must increase because the air takes up space. Volume is the amount of space that matter takes up. If you hold the balloon in one hand and hold a ball of the same size in your other hand, you notice that the ball is heavier. This is because the density of the ball is greater than that of the balloon. Density is the amount of matter in a given volume.

PURPOSE: In this activity, you will learn how to measure the volumes and densities of different solids and liquids.

PROCEDURE

Part A: Mass and Volume of a Rectangular Solid

❑ 1. Use a metric ruler to measure the length, width, and height of a wooden block. Use a wax pencil to label this block *1*. Record your measurements in Table 1 on page 11.

❑ 2. **CALCULATE:** Calculate the volume of block 1, using the following formula.

Volume = length × width × height

Record the volume in Table 1 and in Table 3.

❑ 3. Label the other wooden block *2*. Label the remaining rectangular solids *3* and *4*. In the spaces provided in Tables 1 and 3, indicate what materials solids 3 and 4 are made of.

❑ 4. Repeat Steps 1 and 2 for wooden block 2 and for solids 3 and 4.

❑ 5. Use a triple-beam balance to measure the masses of the wooden blocks and the other rectangular solids. Record the measurements in Table 3.

Part B: Mass and Volume of a Liquid

❑ 1. **MEASURE:** Use the balance to measure the mass of an empty 150-mL beaker. Record the measurement here.

mass of beaker = _____ g

❑ 2. **MEASURE:** Half fill the beaker with water. Place it on the balance and measure the mass of the beaker and water together. Find the mass of the water, using the following formula.

Mass (water) = mass (beaker + water) − mass (beaker)

Record the mass of the water in Table 3.

Materials

100-mL graduated
  cylinder
150-mL beaker
2 rectangular solids of
  the same dimensions
  but different
  materials
2 rectangular wooden
  blocks of different
  dimensions
water
rubbing alcohol
wax pencil
metric ruler
small rock
triple-beam balance

❏ **3.** Pour the water from the beaker into the graduated cylinder. Measure the volume of the water. Remember to read the volume by looking at the bottom of the meniscus. Record the measurement in Table 3.

❏ **4.** Empty the graduated cylinder. Pour the same amount of rubbing alcohol as you had water into the graduated cylinder. Record the volume of rubbing alcohol in Table 3.

❏ **5.** Pour the rubbing alcohol into the beaker. Use the balance to measure the mass of the rubbing alcohol and beaker together. Use the formula in Step 2 to find the mass of the rubbing alcohol. Record the mass of the alcohol in Table 3.

Part C: Mass and Volume of an Irregular Solid

❏ **1.** Half fill the graduated cylinder with water. Read the volume of the water. Record the measurement in Table 2.

❏ **2.** Carefully lower a small rock into the water in the graduated cylinder. The water level should rise. Read the level of the water. Record the volume of the water and rock in Table 2.

❏ **3.** Find the volume of the rock, using the following formula.

Volume (rock) = volume (water + rock) – volume (water)

Because 1 mL = 1 cm^3, you can express the volume of the rock in cm^3.

❏ **4.** Record the volume of the rock in Table 2 and Table 3.

❏ **5.** Use the balance to find the mass of the rock. Record the mass in Table 3.

Part D: Density

❏ **1.** **CALCULATE:** Calculate the density of wooden block 1, using the following formula.

Density = mass (g) ÷ volume (cm^3)

Record the density in Table 3.

❏ **2.** Repeat Step 1 for wooden block 2, rectangular solids 3 and 4, and the rock.

❏ **3.** Calculate the density of water, using the following formula.

Density = mass (g) ÷ volume (mL)

Record the density in Table 3.

❏ **4.** Repeat Step 3 for the rubbing alcohol.

LABORATORY SKILLS WORKSHEET 3 (continued)

OBSERVATIONS

Table 1: Volumes of Rectangular Solids				
Item	Length	Width	Height	Volume
Wooden block 1				cm³
Wooden block 2				cm³
Solid 3 _____				cm³
Solid 4 _____				cm³

Table 2: Volume of an Irregular Solid	
Object	Volume
Water	_____ mL
Water + rock	_____ mL
Rock alone	_____ mL = _____ cm³

Table 3: Mass, Volume, and Density			
Substance	Mass	Volume	Density
Wooden block 1	g	cm³	g/cm³
Wooden block 2	g	cm³	g/cm³
Solid 3 _____	g	cm³	g/cm³
Solid 4 _____	g	cm³	g/cm³
Water	g	cm³	g/cm³
Rubbing alcohol	g	cm³	g/cm³
Rock	g	cm³	g/cm³

1. Which wooden block has the greater volume? Which has the greater mass?

_____

2. How do the densities of the two wooden blocks compare? _____

_____

3. Which rectangular solid—3 or 4—has the greater density? _____

4. Which liquid—water or rubbing alcohol—has the greater density? _____

CONCLUSIONS

5. How is the volume of a rectangular solid measured? _____

_____

6. How is the volume of a liquid measured? _____

_____

7. How is the volume of an irregular solid measured? Why is this method necessary?

_____

_____

_____

8. Can two solids with the same volume have different densities? Explain your

answer. _____

_____

9. Can two solids made of the same substance have different densities? Explain

your answer. _____

_____

10. **COMPARE:** If you filled a 1-L bottle with water and another 1-L bottle with rubbing

alcohol, which bottle would feel heavier? Why? _____

_____

_____

LABORATORY SKILLS WORKSHEET 4

Organizing and Analyzing Data

Materials

paper
pencil

BACKGROUND: Data collected during experiments is not very useful unless it is easy to read and understand. Therefore, scientists often use tables to organize data. A table can display a lot of information in a small space. A table also makes it easy to compare and interpret data. Some tables, such as the one in Figure 1, are very simple and show only a small amount of data. Other tables, such as the one on page 14, are more complex. The type of table you use depends on your data.

PURPOSE: In this activity, you will learn how to make and use tables.

Rainfall	
Day	Amount (cm)
1	0.4
2	0.2
3	1.1
4	1.4
5	0

▲ **Figure 1** A simple table

PROCEDURE

☐ 1. A group of students wanted to see if plants would grow taller when grown with plant food. Three plants were given 10 mL of liquid plant food twice a week. Three other plants were the control group. They were given 10 mL of water twice a week. All other growing conditions were kept the same. Every week for 3 weeks, the students measured the heights of the six plants. Figure 2 shows what one student's lab manual looked like after 3 weeks. Think about how this data could be organized into a table.

☐ 2. **ORGANIZE:** Look at Table 1 on the next page. Like all tables, it has a title. Each column has a heading, and the headings show units for the data. Use the data from the student's lab manual in Figure 2 to complete the table.

Lab Manual

○ *Original height of plants:*
plant 1 = 6.0 cm; plant 2 = 6.5 cm; plant 3 = 6.2 cm;
plant 4 = 6.1 cm; plant 5 – 6.2 cm; plant 6 = 6.3 cm

Height after first week:
plant 1 = 7.5 cm; plant 2 = 8.0 cm; plant 3 = 8.0 cm;
plant 4 = 7.0 cm; plant 5 = 6.8 cm; plant 6 = 6.9 cm

Height after second week:
○ *plant 1 = 9.5 cm; plant 2 = 10.2 cm; plant 3 = 10.1 cm;*
plant 4 = 8.1 cm; plant 5 = 7.7 cm; plant 6 = 8.0 cm

Height after third week:
plant 1 = 11.3 cm; plant 2 = 12.2 cm; plant 3 = 11.3 cm;
plant 4 = 8.9 cm; plant 5 = 8.8 cm; plant 6 = 9.1 cm

▲ **Figure 2** A student collected this data.

OBSERVATIONS

Table 1: Plant Growth					
	Experimental Group			Control Group		
	Height (cm)			Height (cm)		
Week	Plant 1	Plant 2	Plant 3	Plant 4	Plant 5	Plant 6
0						
1						
2						
3						

1. How much did the height of Plant 1 increase during the 3-week period? _____

2. How much did the height of Plant 4 increase during the 3-week period? _____

3. How much did the height of Plant 2 increase in 3 weeks? _____

4. How much did the height of Plant 6 increase in 3 weeks? _____

CONCLUSIONS

5. In general, which group of plants grew more during the 3-week period? _____

6. **ANALYZE:** Do you think that the plant food made the plants grow taller?

   Why or why not? _____

7. Explain how the table made it easier for you to answer the questions you have

   answered so far. _____

8. **ORGANIZE:** Think about the plant growth experiment. How should the table look
   if the students had tested two types of plant food instead of just one, and if they
   had only used two plants for each of the three test groups? On a separate sheet
   of paper, make a table that students could use to present their data.

LABORATORY SKILLS WORKSHEET 5

Graphing

Materials

colored pencils

BACKGROUND: Graphs are a useful way to organize and present information. Graphing data helps you see similarities and patterns. It also helps other people understand your data. Four types of graphs that you can use are line graphs, bar graphs, circle graphs, and pictographs.

PURPOSE: In this activity, you will learn how to make different kinds of graphs.

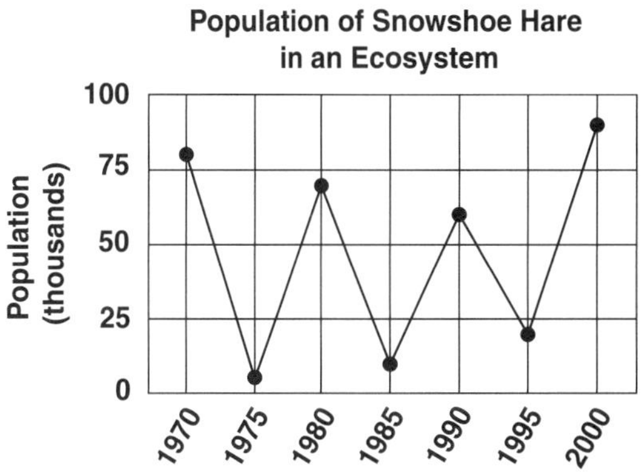

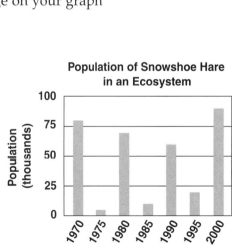

▲ **Figure 1** Line graph

PROCEDURE

Part A: Making a Line Graph

❑ 1. **OBSERVE:** Look at the line graph in Figure 1. Notice that data are plotted as points connected by a line. The horizontal axis shows the range of the independent variable. The vertical axis shows the range of the dependent variable. When graphing, you must decide which values are independent and which are dependent. In Figure 1, the number of hares depends on the year. Therefore, the number of hares is the dependent variable, which goes on the vertical axis. The years go on the horizontal axis.

❑ 2. **GRAPH:** Use the following information and the data in Table 1 to create a line graph in the Observations section on page 17.

> A scientist measured a lizard's body temperature throughout a day. The temperature was 28°C at 8 AM, 31°C at 10 AM, 34°C at 12 noon, 38°C at 2 PM, 36°C at 4 PM, 33°C at 6 PM, and 30°C at 8 PM.

Think about which variable is independent and which is dependent. Remember to include a title and to label the axes. Notice that the low temperature is 28° and the high is 38°. The temperature range on your graph should be from just below this number to just above it.

Part B: Making a Bar Graph

❑ 1. **OBSERVE:** Figure 2 shows a bar graph using the same data as in Figure 1. A bar graph is similar to a line graph except bars rather than points show the data. The bar graph in Figure 2 has the dependent variable on the vertical axis. Bar graphs may also be drawn so that the dependent variable is on the horizontal axis.

❑ 2. **GRAPH:** Use the information about lizard temperature given in Part A Step 2 to create a bar graph in the Observations section. Be sure to label the axes of the graph and to include a title.

Population of Snowshoe Hare in an Ecosystem

▲ **Figure 2** Bar graph

Part C: Making a Circle Graph

❏ 1. **OBSERVE:** Look at the circle graph shown in Figure 3. You can use a circle graph when your data describe parts of a whole. A circle graph is a circle that is divided into sections. The size of each section shows a percentage of the whole circle. Notice that if you add the percentages of the sections together, they equal 100 percent.

❏ 2. If the data are simple, you can draw a circle graph based on simple fractions of a whole. Suppose you want to graph the fractions of birds you see at a pond: 5 ducks, 10 geese, and 5 gulls. Since 5 is 1/4 of the total number of birds, and 10 is 1/2 of the total number of birds, your graph should look like Figure 4.

❏ 3. **GRAPH:** In the Observations section on page 17, draw a circle graph showing the eye colors of students in a class. Assume that there are 24 students in the class: 12 have brown eyes, 8 have blue eyes, and 4 have green eyes. Fill in the three sections using colored pencils to make the graph easier to read. Label the sections and write a title for the graph.

Part D: Making a Pictograph

❏ 1. **OBSERVE:** As the name suggests, a pictograph is a graph using pictures. Look at the pictograph in Figure 5. The percentages of the elements in the human body are represented by the amount of space they occupy on the picture. Figure 6 shows another type of pictograph. In this graph, small pictures represent students with different hair color. The number of students is the dependent variable and is drawn horizontally. The graph could also be drawn with the number of students shown vertically.

❏ 2. **GRAPH:** Make a pictograph in the Observations section showing types of trees found around a school. Use the following data for your graph: 6 elm trees, 3 birch trees, 4 dogwood trees, 7 maple trees, 10 pine trees. Remember to include a title.

Elements in the Human Body

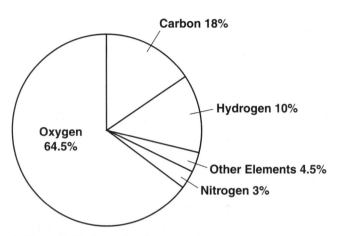

▲ **Figure 3** Circle graph using percentages

Birds Seen at a Pond

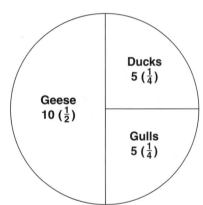

▲ **Figure 4** Circle graph using fractions

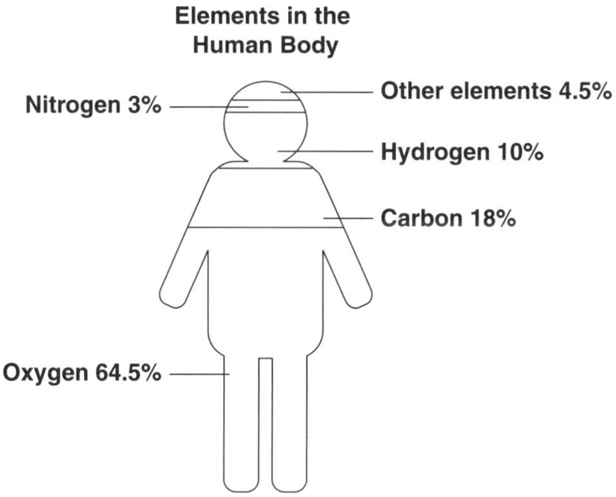

Name _____ Class _____ Date _____

**Elements in the
Human Body**

Nitrogen 3% — Other elements 4.5%

Hydrogen 10%

Carbon 18%

Oxygen 64.5% —

▲ **Figure 5** Pictograph showing percentages

Student Hair Color

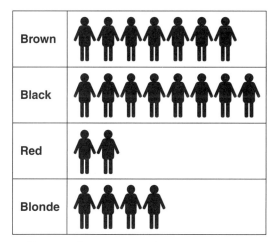

▲ **Figure 6** Pictograph based on numbers

OBSERVATIONS

▲ **Line Graph**

▲ **Bar Graph**

▲ **Circle Graph**

▲ **Pictograph**

CONCLUSIONS

1. What information is presented in the line graph shown in Figure 1? _____ _____

2. What information is presented along the horizontal axis of Figure 1? _____

3. What information is presented along the vertical axis of Figure 2? _____ _____

4. What is the independent variable in Figure 2? What is the dependent variable

   in Figure 2? _____

5. Look at the line graph in Figure 1. What trend do you see in the population of

   snowshoe hare? _____

6. How does the bar graph in Figure 2 show this same trend? _____

7. How would the bar graph shown in Figure 2 look different if the independent
   variable was on the vertical axis instead of on the horizontal axis?

   _____

8. Use the line graph in Figure 1 to determine the population of snowshoe hare in 1975.

   _____

9. What information is shown in the circle graph in Figure 3? _____

10. According to Figure 3, what element makes up most of the human body? What

    percentage of the total body is made up of this element? _____

11. According to Figure 3, what is the combined percentage of oxygen, hydrogen,

    and nitrogen? _____

12. How does a pictograph make data easier to understand compared to using only

    numbers? _____

    _____

LABORATORY SKILLS WORKSHEET 6

Writing a Laboratory Report

Materials
pencil

BACKGROUND: When you perform a laboratory investigation, it is important to keep an organized record of what you do. It is also important to keep an accurate record of your results. An organized record of an investigation is called a laboratory report. A laboratory report is made up of the following sections: Title, Purpose, Background, Hypothesis, Materials, Procedure, Observations, Data, Analysis of Data, and Conclusions.

PURPOSE: In this activity, you will learn how to write a laboratory report.

PROCEDURE

❏ **1.** Study the following descriptions of the sections of a laboratory report.

Title—tells about the experiment
Purpose—reason for doing the experiment
Background—information that will help a reader understand the experiment better
Hypothesis—your idea on what you expect the results of the experiment to be
Materials—list of things needed to perform the experiment
Procedure—steps that will be followed during the experiment
Observations—description of what is seen during the experiment
Data—measurements made during the experiment
Analysis of Data—presentation of the data in tables, charts, graphs, or drawings
Conclusions—summary statement of the results; describes whether the data supported the hypothesis and sources of any errors

> A group of students wanted to investigate the effect of ammonia on seed germination. They suspected that seeds would not germinate very well in water to which ammonia had been added. In order to test their idea, they set up two identical containers filled with soil. In each container, they planted 30 mustard seeds. Both containers were placed near a window.
>
> Every other day, 20 mL of water was added to Container A. A mixture of 10 mL of ammonia and 10 mL of water was added to Container B. The students observed the containers each day to note how many seeds had germinated. After 1 week, 16 seeds had germinated in Container A and 7 seeds had germinated in Container B. After 2 weeks, 28 seeds had germinated in Container A and 13 seeds had germinated in Container B.
>
> Based on their results, the students decided that ammonia has a negative effect on seed germination.

❏ **2.** Reread the experiment described above. Write a possible title for the experiment.

_____

❏ **3.** Notice the data that the students obtained in the experiment. Make a table to record data for the experiment in the Observations section on page 20.

OBSERVATIONS

CONCLUSIONS

1. State the purpose of this experiment in the form of a question. _____

_____

2. What was the hypothesis in this experiment? _____

_____

3. Make a list of materials that the students needed to carry out this experiment.

_____

_____

4. What variable was being tested in this experiment? _____

_____

5. Write a step-by-step procedure for this experiment. _____

_____

_____

_____

_____

6. Write the conclusion that students reached based on their results. _____

_____

LABORATORY CHALLENGE FOR LESSON 1-4

Why do living things need air?

Materials

safety goggles
lab apron
limewater
test tube
graduated cylinder
jar
matches
tongs
stopper (#10)
peanuts
2 watch glasses
drinking straw

BACKGROUND: Burning is a form of oxidation. Oxidation is a chemical reaction in which substances combine with oxygen. Your body gets energy from the oxidation of foods. During oxidation, your body produces carbon dioxide, water vapor, and energy. In order for oxidation to occur, your body must obtain oxygen. You get oxygen from the air you breathe.

PURPOSE: In this activity, you will compare the burning process that goes on in your body with the burning of a substance in air.

PROCEDURE

❏ 1. Put on safety goggles and a lab apron.

❏ 2. Remove a peanut from its shell. Hold the peanut with the tongs.

❏ 3. Have your lab partner light the peanut with a match. ⚠ CAUTION: **Be very careful when lighting and using matches. Be sure to blow out the match immediately after you use it.** Hold the jar upside down. Hold the peanut inside the jar until it stops burning, as shown in Figure 1. ⚠ CAUTION: **Be careful while handling the jar.**

❏ 4. Remove the peanut from the jar and turn the jar right side up.

❏ 5. **MEASURE:** Pour about 2.5 cm of limewater into a graduated cylinder.

❏ 6. **OBSERVE:** Pour the limewater into the jar. Seal the jar with a stopper and shake the jar. Watch what happens to the limewater. Write your observations in Table 1 on page 23.

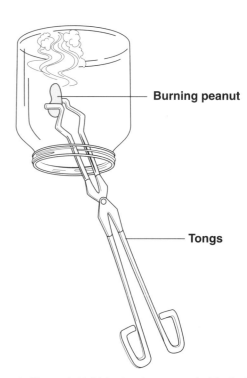

▲ **Figure 1** Hold the burning peanut inside the jar.

❑ 7. **OBSERVE:** Pour limewater into a test tube until it is about one-third full. Place a drinking straw in the test tube, and blow gently into the limewater for about a minute, as shown in Figure 2. Stop to take breaths frequently. ⚠ **CAUTION: Be careful not to take in any limewater through your mouth.** Watch what happens to the limewater. Write your observations in Table 1.

❑ 8. Pick up another peanut with the tongs. Have your lab partner light the peanut with a match. ⚠ **CAUTION: Be careful when lighting the match and working with the burning peanut. Blow out the match immediately after using it.** With your other hand, hold the watch glass upside down over the burning peanut, as shown in Figure 3. ⚠ **CAUTION: Be careful when handling the watch glass.**

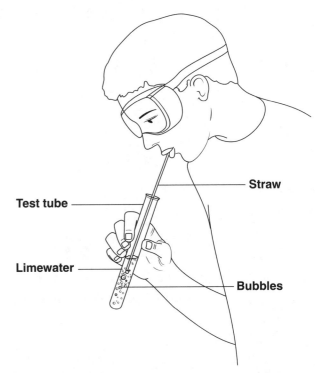

▲ **Figure 2** Blow into the limewater but do not take any into your mouth.

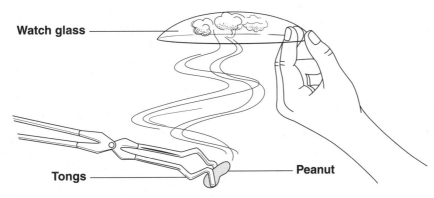

▲ **Figure 3** Hold the watch glass over the burning peanut.

❑ 9. **OBSERVE:** Observe what forms on the watch glass. Write your observations in Table 1.

❑ 10. Hold a clean watch glass and breathe out onto it with your mouth open wide. What material collects on the watch glass? Write your observations in Table 1.

❑ 11. Follow your teacher's instructions to clean up your work area.

LABORATORY CHALLENGE FOR LESSON 1-4 *(continued)*

OBSERVATIONS

Table 1: Comparing Burning Processes	
Situation	**Observation**
Limewater added to bottle after peanut has burned	
Blowing into limewater through straw	
Watch glass held over burning peanut	
Breathing onto watch glass	

1. **INFER:** Limewater is used to test for the presence of carbon dioxide. Limewater turns milky white if it is mixed with carbon dioxide. When was carbon dioxide produced in this activity?

   _____

   _____

2. **INFER:** When was water vapor produced?

   _____

   _____

LABORATORY CHALLENGE FOR LESSON 1-4 *(continued)*

CONCLUSIONS

3. What gas did the peanut use when it burned?

_____

4. Where did this gas come from?

_____

5. **RELATE:** What substances were produced when the peanut burned?

_____

6. How does your body take in oxygen?

_____

_____

7. **RELATE:** What substances are given off when you exhale?

_____

8. **COMPARE:** How is the burning of a peanut similar to the oxidation of food?

_____

_____

_____

LABORATORY CHALLENGE FOR LESSON 2-1

How is a microscope used?

BACKGROUND: A compound microscope consists of two or more lenses. A compound microscope is much more powerful than a simple microscope, which has only one lens. A compound microscope can help you see things much too small to be seen by your eyes alone.

PURPOSE: In this activity, you will learn how to use a compound microscope.

PROCEDURE

❏ **1.** Carry a microscope to your lab table or desk. To carry the microscope, hold it by the arm and the base, as shown in Figure 1. Be very careful when carrying or handling a microscope. Do not touch the lenses with your fingers. Place the microscope on a flat surface with the arm toward you.

❏ **2.** **OBSERVE:** Observe the drawing of a compound microscope in Figure 2. Compare the drawing to your microscope to learn where all the parts are.

❏ **3.** Use a piece of lens paper to gently clean the glass surfaces of the microscope.

Materials

compound microscope
coverslip
lens paper
microscope slide
newspaper
scissors

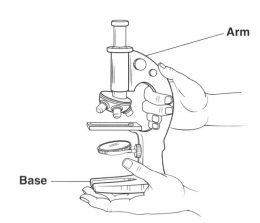

▲ **Figure 1** Carry a microscope by the arm and base.

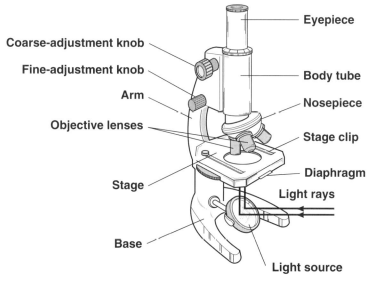

▲ **Figure 2** A compound microscope

❑ **4.** Cut a small letter *e* from a newspaper.

❑ **5.** Place the letter on a clean microscope slide and cover it with a coverslip.
⚠ **CAUTION: Be very careful when handling glass slides.**

❑ **6.** Put the slide on the stage of the microscope. Be sure that the *e* is in the field of view directly over the opening in the stage. Place the clips on the slide to hold it in place.

❑ **7.** Turn the nosepiece so that the low-power objective is in position.

❑ **8.** **OBSERVE:** Lower the body tube slowly, using the coarse-adjustment knob. Watch from the side as you lower the tube and stop when the objective is almost touching the slide. Never let the tube touch the slide.

❑ **9.** **OBSERVE:** Look under the stage of the microscope for the diaphragm. Set the diaphragm at its widest opening to let the most light through.

❑ **10.** **OBSERVE:** Look through the eyepiece of the microscope. Move the mirror slowly until you see a bright circle of light. If your microscope has its own light, turn it on.

❑ **11.** **OBSERVE:** Look into the eyepiece and slowly turn the coarse-adjustment knob to make the tube move upward, as shown in Figure 3. Do not move the tube downward unless you are watching from the side or you might hit the slide and damage the objective.

Coarse-adjustment knob

▲ **Figure 3** Turn the course-adjustment knob to lower the body tube.

❑ **12.** **OBSERVE:** Stop moving the coarse-adjustment knob when the *e* comes into focus. Then, use the fine-adjustment knob to get a sharper image.

❑ **13.** In the space provided in Observations on page 27, make a drawing of the *e* as it appears under the microscope.

❑ **14.** **HYPOTHESIZE:** Repeat Steps 4–13, using two other letters cut from the newspaper. First, hypothesize how the letters will appear when observed through the microscope. Make drawings of your hypothesis. Then, observe the letters.

Name _____ Class _____ Date _____

LABORATORY CHALLENGE FOR LESSON 2-1 *(continued)*

OBSERVATIONS

1. Draw the *e* as it appears under the microscope.

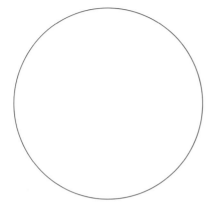

2. Describe how the *e* looks under the microscope.

_____

_____

3. **COMPARE:** In what ways is the appearance of the *e* under the microscope different from the way it looks in the newspaper?

_____

_____

4. **COMPARE:** How do the other letters appear under the microscope? Were your inferences accurate? Draw the letters in the spaces below.

_____

_____

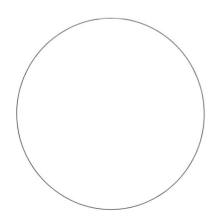 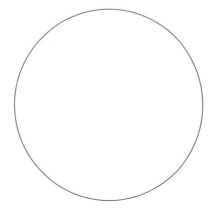

CONCLUSIONS

5. How should you carry a microscope?

_____

_____

6. How do you clean the lenses and mirror of a microscope?

_____

_____

7. To determine the magnification of the specimen, multiply the eyepiece power by the objective power. What magnification did you use? Show your work in the space provided.

magnification = _____

8. Why must you be careful when lowering the tube with the coarse-adjustment knob?

_____

_____

_____

_____

9. Why do you use the fine-adjustment knob?

_____

_____

_____

_____

Name _____ Class _____ Date _____

LABORATORY CHALLENGE FOR LESSON 2-2

What are living things made of?

Materials
Elodea leaf
microscope slides
dropper
water
coverslips
microscope
prepared slide of human
   cheek cells

BACKGROUND: The life functions of a living thing are carried out by its cells. The cells in plants are both similar to and different from the cells in animals.

PURPOSE: In this activity, you will use a microscope to examine some plant and animal cells.

PROCEDURE

❑ 1. Break off a young *Elodea* leaf from the tip of the plant. Place the leaf on a microscope slide.

❑ 2. Use a dropper to place a drop of water on top of the leaf.

❑ 3. Place the coverslip on one edge of the water drop on the slide. Lower the coverslip slowly over the wet leaf, as shown in Figure 1.

❑ 4. **OBSERVE:** Look at the *Elodea* leaf under the low-power objective of the microscope. Remember to lower the objective slowly, using the coarse-adjustment knob. Focus on one of the *Elodea* cells. Look for the cell wall, cytoplasm, and chloroplasts. Sketch the appearance of the *Elodea* leaf in the appropriate circle on page 30.

▲ **Figure 1** Lower a coverslip over the leaf.

❑ 5. **OBSERVE:** Look at the *Elodea* leaf under the high-power objective. Use the fine-adjustment knob to focus. Find the nucleus.

❑ 6. **MODEL:** Sketch the cell as it appears under the high power in the appropriate circle. Label the parts of the *Elodea* cell in your drawing.

❑ 7. **MODEL:** Place a prepared slide of cheek cells on the stage of the microscope. Examine the slide under the low-power objective. Sketch what you observe in the appropriate circle.

❑ 8. **OBSERVE:** Under low power, find a single cheek cell that you can see clearly. Then, switch to high power. Focus the microscope with the fine-adjustment knob.

❑ 9. **MODEL:** Examine the cheek cell carefully. Draw and label a cheek cell in the appropriate circle.

OBSERVATIONS

Elodea Low Power

Elodea High Power

Cheek Cells Low Power

Cheek Cells High Power

1. What is the shape of the *Elodea* cell? _____

2. What is the shape of a cheek cell? _____

3. **IDENTIFY:** What cell parts could you identify in the *Elodea* cell? _____

_____

4. **COMPARE:** What cell parts did you see in both cells? _____

_____

CONCLUSIONS

5. **COMPARE:** How is a plant cell similar to an animal cell? _____

_____

6. **CONTRAST:** How do plant and animal cells differ? _____

_____

_____

LABORATORY CHALLENGE FOR LESSON 2-9

What is mitosis?

Materials

microscope
prepared slide of onion
    root tip

BACKGROUND: New cells form by cell division. A parent cell divides to form two daughter cells. Cell division is controlled by the nucleus. During cell division, the chromosomes make copies of themselves. Then, the nucleus divides. The division of the nucleus is called mitosis. Mitosis occurs in several phases.

PURPOSE: In this activity, you will observe cells in various stages of cell division in an onion root tip.

PROCEDURE

❑ 1. Place a slide of an onion root tip on the stage of the microscope. Adjust the light source or mirror so that you get the best view through the microscope.

❑ 2. Focus the microscope under the low-power objective. Be very careful when lowering the body tube to focus the microscope. Never let the tube hit the slide.

❑ 3. **OBSERVE:** Move the slide slowly until you see the tip of the root. Then, move the slide until you see the cells that are right behind the root cap. Switch to high power. Focus the microscope with the **fine-adjustment knob only.** Look for a cell that is in the first, or resting, phase of cell division. You should be able to see the nucleus clearly. It will appear dark. You will not see any chromosomes. Draw a diagram of this phase in the first circle on page 32. Write the name of this phase in the space provided.

❑ 4. **MODEL:** Look for a cell in which the membrane around the nucleus is faint. Remember to move the slide slowly as you search. You will see chromosomes throughout the nucleus. Draw what you see in the appropriate circle. Write the name of this phase in the space provided.

❑ 5. Find a cell in which the chromosomes are lined up in pairs down the middle of the cell. Make a drawing of this phase in the appropriate circle. Write the name of this phase in the space provided.

❑ 6. Locate a cell in which the pairs of chromosomes have separated. You will see the chromosomes from each pair on opposite sides of the cell. Draw this stage in the appropriate circle. Write the name of this phase in the space provided.

❑ 7. Look for a cell in which the chromosomes are clustered together at opposite ends of the cell. A new cell wall can be seen forming down the middle of the cell. Draw what you see in the appropriate circle. Write the name of this phase in the space provided.

❑ 8. Find a cell in which the new cell wall and cell membranes have completely formed. The nuclei of the cells will appear dark. Make a drawing of what you see in the appropriate circle. Write the name of this phase in the space provided.

OBSERVATIONS

_____   _____   _____

_____   _____   _____

CONCLUSIONS

1. How do cells reproduce? _____

2. What happens during mitosis? _____

3. If a parent cell has 46 chromosomes, how many chromosomes will each daughter cell have?

_____

4. How can each of two daughter cells have the same chromosomes as the parent cell?

_____

_____

_____

LABORATORY CHALLENGE FOR LESSON 3-7

How can incomplete dominance determine traits?

Materials

photocopy of page 36

scissors

BACKGROUND: Incomplete dominance occurs when one allele is not capable of completely determining a trait. In incomplete dominance, offspring show a blending of traits from each parent.

An example of this type of inheritance is found in the alleles that control the color of four o'clock flowers. Four o'clock flowers can have alleles for red coloring or white coloring. The red allele is not completely dominant over the white allele. When you combine the allele for red four o'clock flowers and the allele for white four o'clock flowers, the result will be pink four o'clock flowers.

PURPOSE: In this activity, you will model incomplete dominance in four o'clock flowers.

PROCEDURE

❏ 1. Carefully cut out the eight gene diagrams in Figure 1 from the photocopy of page 36. ⚠ CAUTION: Be careful when using scissors. Each of the diagrams represents coloring alleles for four o'clock flowers. You should have four allele diagrams for red coloring (**R**) and four allele diagrams for white coloring (**W**).

❏ 2. Put two **R** alleles together. See what word is spelled out. This word tells you the color of a four o'clock flower that has two alleles for red coloring.

Write the word here: _____

❏ 3. Put two **W** alleles together. See what word is spelled out. This word tells you the color of a four o'clock flower that has two alleles for white coloring.

Write the word here: _____

❏ 4. Put an **R** allele together with a **W** allele. See what word is spelled out. This word tells you the color of a four o'clock flower that has one allele for red coloring and one allele for white coloring.

Write the word here: _____

❏ 5. **MODEL:** Suppose that a homozygous red four o'clock flower is crossed with another homozygous red four o'clock flower. Make models of the parent flowers by using two **R** allele cards for each parent.

❏ 6. **MODEL:** Use your models to see what possible colors the offspring flowers can be with parents that both have RR alleles. Remember that the offspring will receive one allele from each parent flower. Fill in the Punnett square below with the correct gene combinations for the offspring. Write the possible combinations in the first row of Table 1 on page 35.

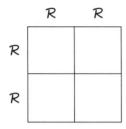

❏ 7. **MODEL:** Repeat Step 6 for two white flowers as parents. Fill in the Punnett square below with the correct gene combinations for the offspring. Write the possible combinations in the second row of Table 1.

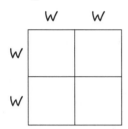

❏ 8. **MODEL:** A pink four o'clock flower has one **R** allele and one **W** allele. Use your allele diagrams to make models of two pink four o'clock flowers. Then, use the diagrams to see what colors the offspring can be if the pink flowers are crossed. Fill in the Punnett square below with the correct gene combinations for the offspring. Write your observations in the third row of Table 1.

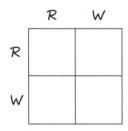

❏ 9. **MODEL:** Suppose that a white four o'clock flower is crossed with a pink four o'clock flower. Use your allele diagrams to see what possible colors the offspring can be. Write your observations in the fourth row of Table 1.

❏10. **APPLY:** Cross a pink four o'clock flower with a red four o'clock flower. See what colors the offspring can be. Write your results in the fifth row of Table 1.

Name _____ Class _____ Date _____

OBSERVATIONS

Table 1: Allele Combinations for Four O'clock Flowers			
Parent 1	Parent 2	Possible Allele Combinations	Possible Color of Offspring
RR	RR		
WW	WW		
RW	RW		
WW	RW		
RW	RR		

CONCLUSIONS

1. **ANALYZE**: Can two white four o'clock flowers have red offspring? Why or why not?

   _____

   _____

   _____

2. **ANALYZE**: Can two pink four o'clock flowers have white offspring? Why or why not?

   _____

   _____

   _____

3. **CONTRAST**: How is inheriting traits by incomplete dominance different from inheriting traits by alleles that are completely dominant and recessive?

   _____

   _____

   _____

   _____

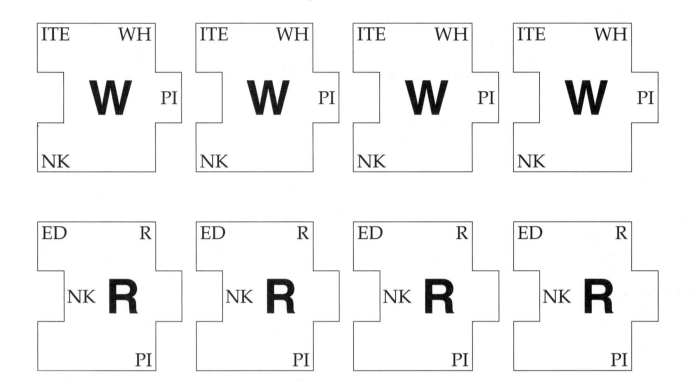

▲ **Figure 1** Allele diagrams for color of four o'clock flowers

Name _____ Class _____ Date _____

How do scientists learn about people from the past?

Materials

paper

pencil

BACKGROUND: Scientists who specialize in the study of humans are called anthropologists. Some anthropologists study the cultures and societies of people who lived long ago. They ask and answer questions such as how people lived, what they wore, what they ate, and what they did for work, and so on. They also seek to explain the social, cultural, and religious behavior of groups of people. Anthropologists have many ways of learning about ancient cultures. One way is to examine the tools and other everyday objects that people of a particular time and place left behind.

PURPOSE: In this activity, you will learn about the types of evidence that anthropologists use when they study people of the past. You will also consider kinds of evidence about your own culture that might be valuable to an anthropologist many years from now.

PROCEDURE

❏ **1.** Figures 1, 2, and 3 illustrate objects that were left behind by three different groups of prehistoric people. Refer to these figures as you continue this activity.

❏ **2.** **ANALYZE:** Look at the objects in Figure 1. In Table 1 on page 38, identify and describe each object as best you can. Also, tell what you think each object might have been used for. If you are not sure about an object, tell what you think it might be or what it reminds you of.

❏ **3.** **ANALYZE:** Repeat Step 2 for the objects in Figures 2 and 3. Write your answers in Tables 2 and 3.

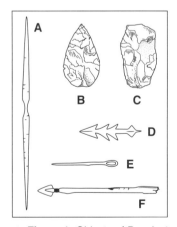

▲ **Figure 1** Objects of People 1

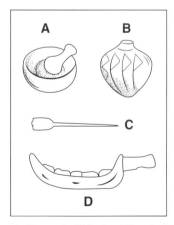

▲ **Figure 2** Objects of People 2

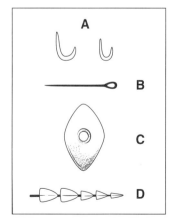

▲ **Figure 3** Objects of People 3

❑ **4. INFER:** Look at question 1 in Table 4. Answer the question based on your analysis of the objects in Figures 1, 2, and 3. Write your answers in the correct spaces.

❑ **5. MODEL:** Repeat Step 4 for each of the remaining questions in Table 4.

OBSERVATIONS

Table 1: Objects of Prehistoric People—Figure 1

Object	Description
A	
B	
C	
D	
E	
F	

Table 2: Objects of Prehistoric People—Figure 2

Object	Description
A	
B	
C	
D	

Table 3: Objects of Prehistoric People—Figure 3

Object	Description
A	
B	
C	
D	

LABORATORY CHALLENGE FOR LESSON 4-6 *(continued)*

Table 4: Describing Prehistoric People			
Question	People 1	People 2	People 3
1. What did they eat?			
2. Did they use fire?			
3. Did they use tools?			
4. Did they farm?			
5. Did they hunt?			
6. Did they fish?			
7. Did they use furs for clothing?			

CONCLUSIONS

1. **COMMUNICATE:** Look at your answers to the questions in Table 4. Choose any two of the questions and explain how you arrived at the conclusions you did.

   _____

   _____

   _____

   _____

2. Write a brief summary about the prehistoric people whose objects were shown in Figure 1.

   _____

   _____

   _____

3. Write a brief summary about the prehistoric people whose objects were shown in Figure 2.

   _____

   _____

   _____

4. Write a brief summary about the prehistoric people whose objects are shown in Figure 3.

_____

_____

_____

5. MODEL: Imagine that objects from your own culture are found on Earth 500,000 years from now. What objects from your daily life would tell an anthropologist what your life was like? In the space below, draw and label four objects that would answer the kinds of questions that anthropologists ask about ancient people.

A

B

C

D

Name _____ Class _____ Date _____

How can you use a dichotomous key to classify organisms?

Materials

paper
pencil

BACKGROUND: Scientists classify organisms according to similarities and differences. One way to group organisms is by using a dichotomous key. The term *dichotomous* means "divided into two parts." A dichotomous key is designed to separate a group of organisms into two smaller groups. These groups are then separated once again into two smaller groups, and so on. Each step in the key involves a yes/no question about the organism's appearance.

PURPOSE: In this activity, you will determine how to use a dichotomous key to classify organisms. You will then make your own dichotomous key.

PROCEDURE

Part A: Using a Dichotomous Key

❑ 1. **OBSERVE:** Carefully observe the six leaves shown in Figure 1.

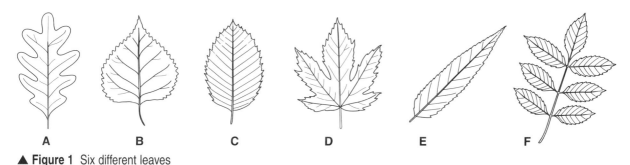

▲ **Figure 1** Six different leaves

❑ 2. **CLASSIFY:** Under each head in Table 1, place a check mark if the leaf you are observing has the characteristic listed. If the leaf does not have the characteristic, leave the space blank.

Table 1: Observing Different Leaves						
Leaf	A	B	C	D	E	F
Leaflets						
Lobes						
Long and narrow shape						
Heart-shaped						
Pointed lobes						

❑ 3. **IDENTIFY:** For each leaf, go through the five questions in Table 2, using the information you gathered in Table 1. Each time you get a yes answer, write your result in Table 3.

Table 2: Dichotomous Key for Leaves		
Question	**Yes**	**No**
1. Is the leaf blade made up of small leaflets?	The leaf is a green ash.	Go to 2.
2. Is the leaf blade long and narrow?	The leaf is a black willow.	Go to 3.
3. Is the leaf blade cut into lobes?	Go to 4.	Go to 5.
4. Are the lobes pointed?	The leaf is a silver maple.	The leaf is a white oak.
5. Is the leaf heart-shaped?	The leaf is a cottonwood.	The leaf is an American elm.

Table 3: Leaf Identification			
Leaf	**Identification**	**Leaf**	**Identification**
A		D	
B		E	
C		F	

Part B: Making a Dichotomous Key

❑ 1. **OBSERVE:** Observe the six animals shown in Figure 2 on page 43.

❑ 2. **CLASSIFY:** Complete Table 4 based on your observations of the animals in Figure 2. Use the same procedure you used for the leaves in Step 2.

❑ 3. **APPLY:** Use what you have learned so far in this activity to make a dichotomous key in Table 5 for the animals in Figure 2. The questions and some of the answers in the key have already been filled in for you. Refer to Table 4 for details about the animals. Your completed key should resemble the key for leaves in Table 2. It should identify each animal.

LABORATORY CHALLENGE FOR LESSON 5-2 *(continued)*

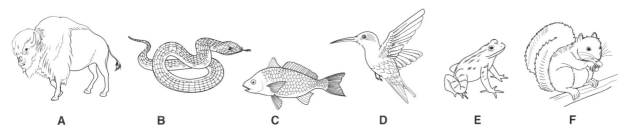

▲ **Figure 2** Six different animals

OBSERVATIONS

Table 4: Observing Different Animals										
Animal	Fins	Wings	Legs		Hooves	Claws	Scales	Feathers	Fur	Smooth Skin
			2	4						
A										
B										
C										
D										
E										
F										

Table 5: Dichotomous Key for Animals		
Question	Yes	No
1. Does the animal have smooth, moist skin?		
2. Does the animal have only two legs?		
3. Does the animal have fur?	Go to 4.	Go to 5.
4. Does the animal have hooves?		
5. Does the animal have fins?		

CONCLUSIONS

1. **INFER:** What makes Tables 2 and 5 dichotomous keys for leaves or animals?

_____

_____

2. **APPLY:** How did the dichotomous keys help you to identify the leaves in Figure 1 and the animals in Figure 2?

_____

_____

CRITICAL THINKING

3. **RELATE:** How would using a dichotomous key be useful to a scientist studying different kinds of insects?

_____

_____

4. **APPLY:** What other items could be classified by using a dichotomous key?

_____

_____

LABORATORY CHALLENGE FOR LESSON 6-6

How do yeast cells reproduce?

BACKGROUND: During baking, yeast cells break down carbohydrates in the bread dough. Yeast is actually a living, one-celled organism. Yeast cells reproduce asexually.

PURPOSE: In this activity, you will observe how yeast cells reproduce. You will also observe the activity of yeast cells as they break down carbohydrates.

PROCEDURE

☐ 1. Put on safety goggles and a lab apron.

☐ 2. **MEASURE:** Use a graduated cylinder to measure 50 mL of limewater. Pour the limewater into an Erlenmeyer flask and set the flask aside. Using a wax pencil, label the flask *A*. Limewater turns milky when it is mixed with carbon dioxide. You will use limewater in this activity to indicate that carbon dioxide is being produced.

☐ 3. **MEASURE:** Rinse the graduated cylinder. Then, use it to measure 60 mL of very warm water into the other Erlenmeyer flask. Label this flask *B*. Next, use the graduated cylinder to measure 6 mL of corn syrup. Swirl the flask to dissolve the corn syrup in the water. This will make a sugar solution.

☐ 4. **MEASURE:** Add half of a package of dry yeast to the sugar solution to form a yeast culture. Swirl the solution around gently. Rinse the graduated cylinder again. Then, use it to measure about 2 mL of the solution. Pour this into a small beaker and put it aside for use in Step 7.

☐ 5. Attach one end of the rubber tubing to the glass tubing in the stopper, as shown in Figure 1. ⚠ **CAUTION: Be very careful when working with glass tubing.** Place the stopper with the glass tubing into Flask B.

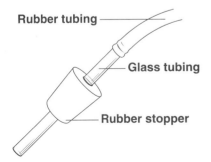

▲ **Figure 1** Attach the rubber tubing to the glass tubing.

Materials

safety goggles

lab apron

gloves

100-mL graduated cylinder

limewater

150-mL Erlenmeyer flasks (2)

wax pencil

10-mL graduated cylinders (2)

warm water

corn syrup

dry yeast

small beaker

one-hole rubber stopper (#5) with 10-cm glass tubing

40-cm length of rubber tubing

dropper

microscope slide

methylene blue

coverslip

paper towel

microscope

❏ **6.** Put the other end of the rubber tubing into Flask A, which contains the limewater, as in Figure 2. Be sure that the end of the rubber tubing is below the surface of the limewater, as shown in Figure 2. Set the two flasks aside.

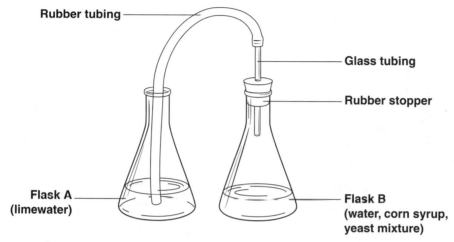

Rubber tubing
Glass tubing
Rubber stopper
Flask A (limewater)
Flask B (water, corn syrup, yeast mixture)

▲ **Figure 2** Flasks with sugar solution and limewater

❏ **7.** Put on gloves. Use a dropper to place a drop of the yeast culture onto a microscope slide. Add a drop of methylene blue. Place the coverslip over the culture. Use a paper towel to absorb excess methylene blue that seeps out around the coverslip. The methylene blue stains the cell nuclei so that you can see them. ⚠ **CAUTION: Methylene blue can stain your clothing and skin.**

❏ **8.** Remove your safety goggles. Place the slide under your microscope and focus the microscope under the low-power objective. Then, focus the microscope under the high-power objective. Always look at the slide from the side when lowering the objective to avoid damaging the lens or the slide.

❏ **9. OBSERVE:** Look for a yeast cell that has a bud on it. First, look for the cell wall. Then, find the nucleus in the daughter cell. Draw and label what you see in the space provided in Figure 3 on page 47.

❏ **10.** Find a yeast cell that is just beginning to form a bud. Draw and label this cell in the space for Figure 4.

❏ **11. OBSERVE:** Go back and look at the two flasks that you set up in Steps 1–6. Observe the flasks carefully. Look at the limewater in the flask. Write your observations in Table 1 on page 47.

❏ **12.** Rinse the beaker containing the yeast culture as well as the slide and coverslip you used to observe the yeast culture under the microscope. Prepare a fresh yeast culture in the beaker, using 30 mL of very warm water, 6 mL of corn syrup, and half of a package of yeast.

LABORATORY CHALLENGE FOR LESSON 6-6 *(continued)*

☐ 13. **OBSERVE:** Repeat Steps 7 and 8 for viewing the yeast culture under the microscope. Notice the difference in the number of yeast cells that you see when you look at a freshly made yeast culture. Observe whether there are any yeast cells with buds.

☐ 14. Follow your teacher's instructions to clean up your work area. Wash your hands thoroughly.

OBSERVATIONS

▲ **Figure 3** Yeast cell with bud

▲ **Figure 4** Yeast cell beginning to form bud

Table 1: Observing the Activity of Yeast	
Question	**Observation**
What is happening in the flask with yeast?	
What is the color of the limewater?	

1. **INFER:** What is causing the activity in Flask B?

_____

_____

2. INFER: What caused the limewater to change color?

_____

_____

3. COMPARE: How did the number of yeast cells you saw on the microscope slide in the freshly made yeast culture differ from the number you saw in the yeast culture that was several minutes old? Explain.

_____

_____

_____

4. OBSERVE: Did you notice any yeast cells with buds in the freshly made yeast culture? Explain.

_____

_____

CONCLUSIONS

5. ANALYZE: How do the yeast cells you studied in this lab reproduce?

_____

6. IDENTIFY: What gas is produced as yeast cells break down carbohydrates?

_____

7. IDENTIFY: What was the source of carbohydrates in this investigation?

_____

CRITICAL THINKING

8. APPLY: Explain how the activity of yeast is useful in baking bread.

_____

_____

_____

LABORATORY CHALLENGE FOR LESSON 7-2

How do moisture and light affect moss growth?

Materials

8 medium-sized paper
cups

soil

8 clumps of fresh moss

marking pen

water

hand lens

BACKGROUND: Mosses are simple, nonvascular plants. They grow close together, forming what look like soft, green mats in sidewalk cracks, on rocks, along the sides of buildings, and at the bases of trees. They lack true roots, but have threadlike structures that anchor the plant to a surface, as roots anchor most other plants.

PURPOSE: In this activity, you will observe how moisture and light affect moss growth.

PROCEDURE

❏ **1.** Obtain eight clumps of moss with enough soil in which to grow the moss specimens.

❏ **2.** Fill the eight paper cups with soil. Plant a clump of moss in each cup as shown.

❏ **3.** Label cups 1 and 2 *Water* and *Sun.* Label cups 3 and 4 *Little Water* and *Sun.*

❏ **4.** Label cups 5 and 6 *Water* and *Shade.* Label cups 7 and 8 *Little Water* and *Shade.*

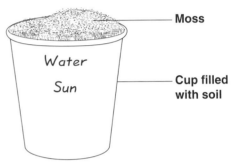

▲ **Figure 1** Plant a clump of moss in each cup.

❏ **5.** Place cups 1, 2, 3, and 4 in an area where the moss plants will receive direct sunlight for most of the day. Place cups 5, 6, 7, and 8 in an area where the moss plants will receive indirect sunlight for part of the day and will be shaded the rest of the day.

❏ **6.** Follow your teacher's instructions for cleaning up your work area. Wash your hands thoroughly.

❏ **7.** Water the plants in cups 1, 2, 5, and 6 every day. Be sure to give each plant the same amount of water.

❏ **8.** Water the plants in cups 3, 4, 7, and 8 only once, after 3 days have passed. Be sure to give each plant the same amount of water.

❏ **9.** **HYPOTHESIZE:** What effect do you think direct sunlight will have on the plants? What effect do you think limited water will have on the plants?

_____

_____

❏**10.** **PREDICT:** Predict which of the eight plants will grow the best. _____
To test your prediction, continue the investigation.

❏**11.** **OBSERVE:** After 4–5 days, examine the moss plants with a hand lens. Observe the growth of each plant. Write your observations in Table 1 on page 50.

OBSERVATIONS

Table 1: Moss Plant Observations		
Plant Numbers	**Conditions**	**Observations**
1, 2	water, Sun	
3, 4	little water, Sun	
5, 6	water, shade	
7, 8	little water, shade	

CONCLUSIONS

1. **IDENTIFY:** What are the variables being tested in this experiment?

_____

2. **IDENTIFY:** What combinations of these variables are being tested?

_____

_____

3. **INFER:** Why do you think two cups of moss were used for each growth

condition? _____

_____

4. **COMPARE:** Which plants grew best? Which plants grew second best?

_____

_____

5. **ANALYZE:** Was your hypothesis correct? Use your observations to support your

answer. _____

_____

6. **HYPOTHESIZE:** What environmental conditions are best for the growth of moss

plants? _____

_____

LABORATORY CHALLENGE FOR LESSON 8-9

How do green plants reproduce asexually?

Materials

carrot
plastic knife
4 toothpicks
2 clear plastic cups
water
marking pen
metric ruler
geranium plant

BACKGROUND: Some plants can reproduce asexually without seeds. The roots, stems, and leaves of such plants can develop into complete new plants by themselves. This is called vegetative propagation. Some plants undergo vegetative propagation naturally. For example, white potatoes grow from tubers, and onions grow from bulbs. Other plants can grow by artificial vegetative propagation. Growing plants from root, stem, or leaf cuttings is an example of artificial vegetative propagation. For example, a carrot is a large storage root. It can grow new stems and leaves when placed in water.

PURPOSE: In this activity, you will observe two examples of vegetative propagation.

PROCEDURE

Part A: Root Cutting

☐ 1. Cut the bottom half off a carrot. Make the cut at the angle shown in Figure 1. ⚠ **CAUTION: Be careful when using a knife.**

☐ 2. Stick four toothpicks into the sides of the top part of the carrot, as shown in Figure 1.

☐ 3. Fill a plastic cup about three-quarters full of water.

☐ 4. Rest the toothpicks with the carrot on the rim of the cup, as shown in Figure 1. About half of the carrot should be underwater. Add more water if you need to. Mark the water level on the cup. Place the cup where it can remain undisturbed and receive bright sunlight.

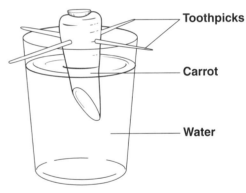

▲ **Figure 1** Use toothpicks to support the carrot.

☐ 5. Follow your teacher's instructions for cleaning up your work area. Wash your hands thoroughly.

☐ 6. **OBSERVE:** Observe the carrot every day for the next 4 weeks. Observe any parts of the carrot that are growing. Record your observations in Table 1. Before the 4 weeks are up, you will need to continue the table on additional paper.

☐ 7. Add more water each day as needed.

☐ 8. **MEASURE:** Every 4 days, measure any growth of new parts you observe. Record the data in Table 1. If there is no growth, write *no growth.*

Part B: Stem Cutting

☐ 1. Cut the stem off a geranium just below a leaf node. Remove the bottom leaves.

☐ 2. Stand the stem up in a cup of water as shown. Mark the water level. Be sure that the leaf nodes are underwater. Place the plant in an area where it can remain undisturbed and receive bright but indirect sunlight.

☐ 3. **OBSERVE:** Observe any new parts that you see growing every day for the next 4 weeks. Add more water as needed.

☐ 4. **MEASURE:** Every 4 days, carefully remove the geranium from the water and measure its longest root. Record the length in Table 2. Before the 4 weeks are up, you will need to continue the table on additional paper.

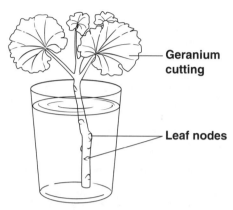

Geranium cutting

Leaf nodes

▲ **Figure 2** Be sure that the leaf nodes are underwater.

OBSERVATIONS

Table 1: Growth From a Root Cutting—Carrot			
Date	**Length of Stem (cm)**	**Date**	**Length of Stem (cm)**

Table 2: Growth From a Stem Cutting—Geranium			
Date	**Length of Longest Root (cm)**	**Date**	**Length of Longest Root (cm)**

LABORATORY CHALLENGE FOR LESSON 8-9 *(continued)*

1. **IDENTIFY:** What growth did you first observe in the carrot?

   _____

2. **IDENTIFY:** What structure appeared second in the carrot?

   _____

3. **IDENTIFY:** What structure began to grow first from the geranium cutting?

   _____

4. **ORGANIZE:** Use the measurements you recorded in Table 1 to graph the growth of the carrot stem. Use the graph below.

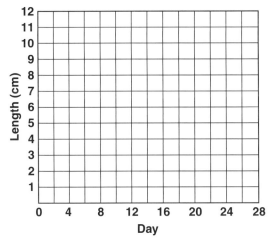

▲ **Figure 3** Growth of carrot stem

5. **ORGANIZE:** Use the measurements you recorded in Table 2 to graph the growth of the geranium root. Use the graph below.

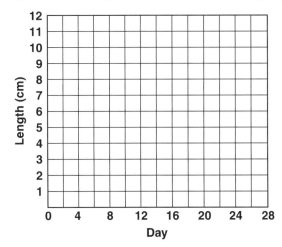

▲ **Figure 4** Growth of geranium root

CONCLUSIONS

6. **CONTRAST:** How does asexual reproduction differ from sexual reproduction?

_____

_____

7. **DESCRIBE:** How does a carrot reproduce asexually?

_____

_____

8. **DESCRIBE:** How can a geranium reproduce asexually?

_____

_____

9. **DESCRIBE:** How does vegetative propagation occur?

_____

_____

LABORATORY CHALLENGE FOR LESSON 9-10

How do insects develop?

Materials

mealworm culture
petri dish
hand lens
forceps

BACKGROUND: Insects go through several stages of development as they mature. The changes that take place are called metamorphosis. In one kind of metamorphosis, the insect that comes out of a hatched egg looks like a small version of the adult. It is called a nymph. Grasshoppers and roaches undergo this kind of metamorphosis.

Some insects come out of the hatched egg as a larva. The larva usually does not look anything like the adult. For example, a caterpillar is the larva of the butterfly. A larva grows rapidly for a while and then begins a resting stage in which it is called a pupa. Following this resting stage, the adult insect emerges.

PURPOSE: In this activity, you will observe the metamorphosis of the mealworm, which is the larva of the tenebrio beetle.

PROCEDURE

- ☐ 1. **OBSERVE:** Examine a mealworm culture in a petri dish, as shown in Figure 1. Use the hand lens to get a better look. Do you see any eggs? If so, what do they look like? Write your observations in Table 1 on page 56. Use Figure 2 as a guide.

- ☐ 2. **OBSERVE:** Examine some of the larvae. Use forceps to handle them. What do the larva look like? Write your observations in Table 1.

- ☐ 3. **OBSERVE:** As mealworms grow, they shed their old skins. Can you find any empty skins in the culture? Record your observations in Table 1.

- ☐ 4. **COMPARE:** Find a mealworm in the pupal stage. Does the pupa seem active or inactive? How does it look compared to the larvae? Write your observations in Table 1.

- ☐ 5. **CONTRAST:** Examine an adult tenebrio beetle with your hand lens. Look for ways in which the beetle is different from its larva. Notice its color, number of legs, level of activity, and other features. Write your observations in Table 1.

- ☐ 6. Follow your teacher's instructions for disposing of materials and cleaning up your work area.

- ☐ 7. Wash your hands thoroughly.

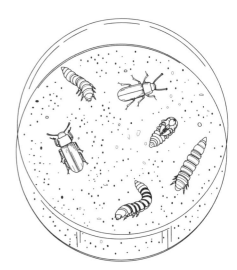

▲ **Figure 1** Mealworm culture

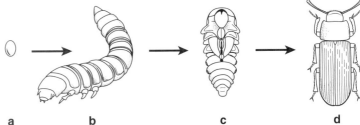

▲ **Figure 2** Tenebrio beetle in its (a) egg, (b) larva, (c) pupa, and (d) adult stages

a   b   c   d

OBSERVATIONS

Table 1: Observing a Mealworm Culture		
Item	Present (yes or no)	Observations
Eggs		
Larva		
Skins		
Pupa		
Adult beetles		

CONCLUSIONS

1. **DESCRIBE:** What is metamorphosis? _____

   _____

   _____

2. **DESCRIBE:** What happens during incomplete metamorphosis? _____

   _____

   _____

3. **DESCRIBE:** What happens during complete metamorphosis? _____

   _____

   _____

4. **APPLY:** Does the tenebrio beetle undergo complete or incomplete metamorphosis? Explain your answer.

   _____

   _____

Name _____ Class _____ Date _____

What are the parts of a feather?

Materials

down feather

contour feather

hand lens

toothpick

BACKGROUND: A body covering of feathers is a special characteristic of birds. Birds have several different kinds of feathers. Down feathers, which are small and fluffy, lie close to a bird's body. These feathers insulate the body and protect a bird from cold weather. Larger contour feathers cover almost the whole bird, over the layer of down. Contour feathers give a bird its color and help it to fly.

PURPOSE: In this activity, you will examine two different types of bird feathers and identify their parts.

PROCEDURE

❑ 1. **COMPARE:** You will receive two feathers. One is a down feather, and one is a contour feather. Examine them carefully. Compare your feathers with the drawings shown in Figure 1.

❑ 2. **MODEL:** Decide which of your feathers is a down feather. Make a drawing of the down feather in the space labeled Diagram 1 on page 58.

❑ 3. **MODEL:** Decide which of your feathers is a contour feather. Make a drawing of the contour feather in the space labeled Diagram 2.

❑ 4. **MODEL:** On both of the feathers you have drawn, label the shaft and vane.

❑ 5. **OBSERVE:** Use the hand lens to observe the vane of each feather. Look closely at the barbs. Use a toothpick to separate the barbs. Locate the barbules that hook the barbs together.

❑ 6. **OBSERVE:** Slowly pull each feather between your thumb and forefinger. Use the hand lens to observe what happens. Write your observations here:

_____

_____

_____

❑ 7. Follow your teacher's instructions for putting away materials.

❑ 8. Wash your hands thoroughly.

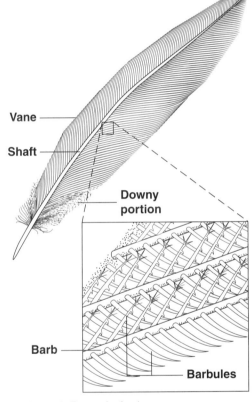

▲ **Figure 1** Parts of a feather

OBSERVATIONS

▲ **Diagram 1** Down feather

▲ **Diagram 2** Contour feather

CONCLUSIONS

1. **ANALYZE:** How is the structure of a down feather adapted to its function of keeping a bird warm?

   _____

   _____

2. **ANALYZE:** How is the structure of a contour feather adapted for flight?

   _____

   _____

3. **INFER:** Birds groom their feathers in a process called preening. This eliminates gaps in the vanes of feathers. Why do you think birds preen themselves?

   _____

   _____

4. **INFER:** Is the shaft of a contour feather solid or hollow? Why does it have this structure?

   _____

   _____

Name _____ Class _____ Date _____

LABORATORY CHALLENGE FOR LESSON 11-2

What is an ecosystem?

Materials

safety goggles
aquarium
plastic knife
2 petri dishes
hand lens
2 plastic pipettes
microscope slide
coverslip
microscope
test tube
test-tube rack
aquarium water
limewater
rubber stopper
thermometer

BACKGROUND: An ecosystem is made up of all the living and nonliving things in an environment. The plant and animal populations within an ecosystem form a community. Sunlight adds energy to an ecosystem. Green plants use the energy in sunlight to make their own food. Plants store the energy as sugars and starches. Because they produce their own food, green plants are called producers. Consumers get energy by eating green plants or other organisms that eat green plants. Decomposers break down the remains of dead organisms.

PURPOSE: In this activity, you will study an aquarium, which is a small ecosystem.

PROCEDURE

☐ 1. **OBSERVE:** Observe the living community within the aquarium. Notice the different types and numbers of organisms present.

☐ 2. **CLASSIFY:** What organisms do you see? List them in Table 1 on page 61. Classify each organism as a producer, a consumer, or a decomposer. Include the number of organisms you see.

☐ 3. Scrape the inside wall of the aquarium with a plastic knife, as shown in Figure 1. Place some of the material scraped off into a petri dish.

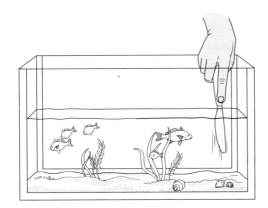

▲ **Figure 1** Scrape material from the aquarium wall.

☐ 4. **OBSERVE:** Examine the material in the dish with a hand lens. What organisms do you observe? Add these organisms to your list in Table 1.

☐ 5. Place a small amount of the material from the aquarium wall onto a microscope slide. Place a coverslip on top of the material. Examine the slide under a microscope, using the low-power objective. What organisms do you observe? Add your observations to the list in Table 1.

❑ **6.** Use a plastic pipette to collect some material from the bottom of the aquarium, as shown in Figure 2. Transfer the material you collected to a clean petri dish.

❑ **7.** **OBSERVE:** Use the pipette to place a drop of the material from the dish onto a microscope slide, as shown in Figure 3. Place a coverslip on top of the material. Examine the slide under a microscope, using the low-power objective. What organisms do you observe? Add your observations to the list in Table 1.

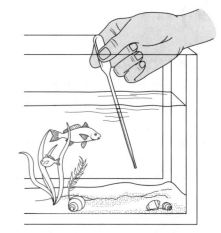

▲ **Figure 2** Collect material from the bottom of the aquarium.

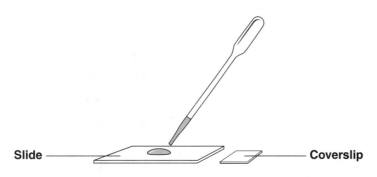

Slide ——————————————————— Coverslip

▲ **Figure 3** Prepare a slide of material from the bottom of the aquarium.

❑ **8.** **OBSERVE:** Examine the slide, using the high-power objective. What other organisms do you observe? Add these observations to the list in Table 1.

❑ **9.** In the circle labeled Diagram 1, draw one of the organisms that you observed while using the microscope.

❑ **10.** Place a test tube in a test-tube rack. Use your pipette to half fill the test tube with aquarium water.

❑ **11.** Fill a clean pipette with limewater and add this to the test tube. Seal the test tube with a rubber stopper and shake it. What do you observe?

_____

_____

❑ **12.** Follow your teacher's instructions for cleaning up your work area. Wash your hands thoroughly.

▲ **Diagram 1**

LABORATORY CHALLENGE FOR LESSON 11-2 *(continued)*

OBSERVATIONS

Table 1: The Aquarium Community					
Producers		Consumers		Decomposers	
Kind	How many?	Kind	How many?	Kind	How many?

1. **CLASSIFY:** How can you tell which organisms in the aquarium are producers and which organisms are consumers?

_____

_____

2. **INFER:** Based on your addition of limewater to the aquarium water, what gas is present in the aquarium water?

_____

CONCLUSIONS

3. **IDENTIFY:** What are some of the organisms that make up the aquarium community?

_____

_____

4. **INFER:** What are some of the materials that are recycled in this ecosystem?

_____

_____

5. **INFER:** What is the primary source of energy for this ecosystem?

_____

6. **IDENTIFY:** Which organisms use and store this energy directly?

_____

_____

7. **INFER:** Explain how some organisms in the aquarium get their energy indirectly.

_____

_____

CRITICAL THINKING

8. **INFER:** Is this ecosystem self-sustaining (able to keep up its activity on its own)? Why or why not?

_____

_____

_____

Name _____ Class _____ Date _____

How does energy pass through a food web?

BACKGROUND: Organisms in an ecosystem transfer energy and nutrients through the food they eat. A food chain shows how energy and nutrients move from one organism to another in an ecosystem. Because most organisms eat more than one type of food, they are part of more than one food chain. A food web is a network of food chains in an ecosystem. Depending on how they get nutrients and energy, organisms in an ecosystem can be considered producers, consumers, or decomposers.

PURPOSE: In this activity, you will determine how energy is transferred from one organism to another in food chains and food webs.

PROCEDURE

☐ **1. OBSERVE:** Look at the energy pyramid in Figure 1. It shows the energy available to organisms at each level. Notice that the amount of available energy decreases as you move up the pyramid.

☐ **2. OBSERVE:** Look at the organisms in Table 1 on page 64. Notice that most of the organisms eat other organisms to obtain food and energy. Think about other organisms they might get energy from.

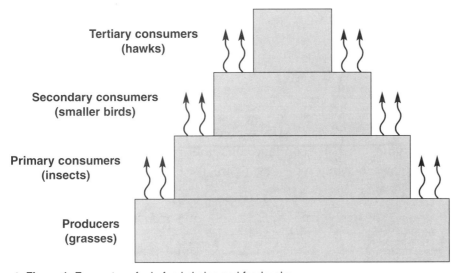

▲ **Figure 1** Energy transfer in food chains and food webs

Table 1: Transfer of Energy Through an Ecosystem	
Organism	**Possible Energy Sources**
Bacteria	dead plants and animals
Bear	fish, shrub berries, insects
Deer	tree needles, leaves, shrub berries
Eagle	rabbits, fish, small animals such as weasels
Earthworm	decomposing matter
Fish	marine plants, other fish
Grass	sun
Insect	leaves
Lynx	animals such as weasels, rabbits, squirrels
Mushroom	dead plants and animals
Rabbit	grass, twigs, bark, fruits
Shrub	sun
Small bird	pinecones, earthworms, insects
Squirrel	tree bark and seeds, shrub berries, insects
Tree (leaves, bark, seeds)	Sun
Weasel	earthworms, small birds, insects, animals such as rabbits and squirrels
Wolf	small birds, fish, animals such as deer, rabbits, and squirrels

❏ 3. **IDENTIFY:** Look at the organisms in Table 1 that have the Sun as their only energy source. What do they have in common?

_____

❏ 4. **CLASSIFY:** Use the information in the table to classify each organism as a producer (*P*), a primary consumer (*PC*), a secondary consumer or higher (*SC*), or a decomposer (*D*). Remember that most organisms feed on a variety of other organisms.

_____ bacteria   _____ earthworm   _____ mushroom   _____ squirrel

_____ bear   _____ grass   _____ rabbit   _____ tree

_____ deer   _____ insect   _____ shrub   _____ weasel

_____ eagle   _____ lynx   _____ small bird   _____ wolf

LABORATORY CHALLENGE FOR LESSON 12-3 *(continued)*

OBSERVATIONS

1. **ANALYZE:** Look at Figure 1 on page 63. Is energy lost or gained as you move up each step of the energy pyramid?

   _____

2. **IDENTIFY:** Use the information in Table 1 to draw a food chain for energy transfer from grass to a wolf in the space below. Remember to include the energy source for the grass. Use Figure 2 as an example.

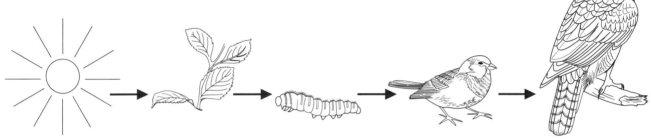

▲ **Figure 2** A simple food chain

3. **IDENTIFY:** Draw a food chain for energy transfer from a tree to an eagle. Remember to include the energy source for the tree.

4. **SYNTHESIZE:** Use the information in Table 1 to draw a food web that includes several plants and animals in this ecosystem. Remember that a food web includes several interconnected food chains. You do not have to use all of the animals in the table.

CONCLUSIONS

5. **INFER:** Figure 1 shows that only a small percentage of an organism's energy is transferred to the next level in a food chain. What happens to the remaining energy?

_____

_____

6. **INFER:** Why are there usually many more primary consumers in an ecosystem than secondary consumers, and many more secondary consumers than higher consumers?

_____

_____

7. **HYPOTHESIZE:** How could a change in the seasons affect the food web you drew for item 4?

_____

_____

_____

LABORATORY CHALLENGE FOR LESSON 13-4

What are the parts of a bone?

BACKGROUND: Bones differ in size and shape. Some, such as ear bones, are small and delicate. Others, such as leg bones, are large and sturdy. All bones have a similar structure and are made of both living and nonliving material. Bones have a thin outer membrane that protects them. The cells in this outer membrane are closely packed, making the bone look smooth. Just inside this membrane is a hard, dense layer that provides strength and support. Most bones also have an inner spongy layer that contains living tissues, such as blood vessels and bone marrow. The spongy layer also provides strength and support.

PURPOSE: In this activity, you will compare the structure of two types of bones.

PROCEDURE

❏ **1.** Put on safety goggles, a lab apron, and gloves.

❏ **2.** **OBSERVE:** Use chalk to observe the effect of hydrochloric acid on calcium. Chalk is made of calcium carbonate. Place a piece of chalk in a small dish. Use a dropper to place several drops of dilute hydrochloric acid on the chalk, as shown in Figure 1. ⚠ **CAUTION: Work carefully to avoid spilling acid on your skin or clothing. If you do spill acid, rinse the area with plenty of water and tell your teacher immediately.** Record your observations here:

_____

_____

_____

_____

▲ **Figure 1** Test the chalk with hydrochloric acid.

❏ **3.** Obtain a beef bone section that has been cut along its length and width, as shown in Figure 2. Lay the bone on its side in a petri dish. Make a simple drawing of the bone in the space labeled Diagram 1.

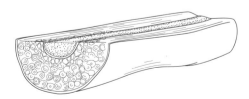

▲ **Figure 2** Beef bone section

❏ 4. **OBSERVE:** Place the bone in the dish so that the outside is facing up. Use the dropper to put several drops of hydrochloric acid on the outer part of the bone. Notice the effect that the acid has on this part of the bone. Record your observations in Table 1.

❏ 5. Hold the bone with tongs and rinse the acid off the bone with plenty of water.

❏ 6. **OBSERVE:** Use tongs to lay the bone in the dish so that the interior of the bone is facing up. Place several drops of acid on the inner part of the bone. Notice any effect that this has on the bone. Record your observations in Table 1.

❏ 7. Using tongs, rinse the acid off the bone with plenty of water.

❏ 8. **RECORD:** Use a plastic knife to scrape away some of the bone, as shown in Figure 3. Try to scrape one area on the outside of the bone and another area on the inside part of the bone. List each area that you scrape in Table 1. Record the texture and hardness of the bone in each area.

❏ 9. **OBSERVE:** Use a hand lens to observe the inside of the bone. Notice the color of the different parts and whether the parts seem smooth or rough. Draw what you see in the space labeled Diagram 2.

❏ 10. **COMPARE:** Compare the structure of the beef bone to the human bone shown in your textbook.

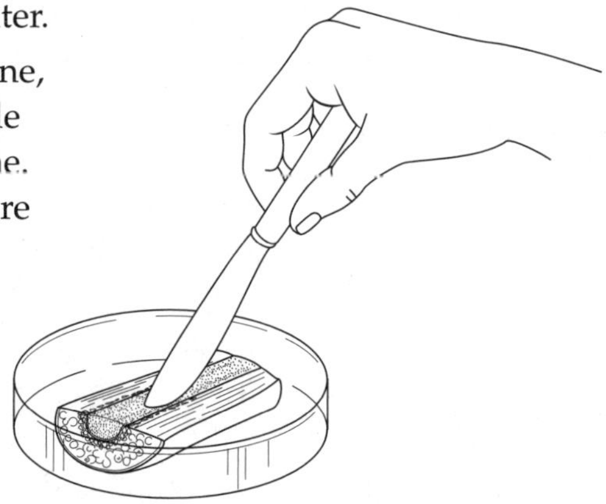

▲ **Figure 3** Scrape the beef bone.

❏ 11. Follow your teacher's instructions for cleaning up your work area. Remove and dispose of your gloves.

OBSERVATIONS

Table 1: Observing a Beef Bone	
Action	**Observations**
Acid on outer part of bone	
Acid on inner part of bone	
Scraping outside of bone	
Scraping inside of bone	

Name _____ Class _____ Date _____

▲ Diagram 1

▲ Diagram 2

1. **INFER:** Does the beef bone contain calcium? How do you know?

   _____

   _____

2. **IDENTIFY:** Which part of the bone seems to contain the most calcium?

   _____

3. **INFER:** Does the beef bone have the same texture and hardness in all places that you scraped? Explain your answer.

   _____

   _____

   _____

4. **COMPARE:** How does the color of the bone's inside part compare with the color of its outside part?

   _____

   _____

5. **COMPARE:** How do the inside and outside of the beef bone compare to the inside and outside of a human bone?

_____

_____

_____

CONCLUSIONS

6. **DESCRIBE:** Explain the difference in color that you observed between the inside and outside parts of the bone.

_____

_____

_____

7. **INFER:** Based on your observations, what mineral do you think gives a bone much of its strength?

_____

_____

8. **INFER:** Red blood cells are produced in the bones of healthy people. In what part of the bone that you observed do you think this production occurs?

_____

_____

_____

CRITICAL THINKING

9. **PREDICT:** Osteoporosis is a bone disorder in which the bones do not have enough calcium. Based on what you learned in this activity, predict how not getting enough calcium could affect bones.

_____

_____

_____

LABORATORY CHALLENGE FOR LESSON 14-2

How is milk digested?

BACKGROUND: Like most foods, milk must be digested before the body's cells can use it. An enzyme called rennin plays an important role in the digestion of milk.

PURPOSE: In this activity, you will learn about the digestion of milk by observing how the enzyme rennin affects it.

PROCEDURE

❑ **1.** Use a wax pencil to label the test tubes *1, 2, 3,* and *4.* Fill three test tubes about one-third full with milk.

❑ **2.** **RECORD:** Using a funnel, add about a tablespoon of powdered Junket, which is your source of rennin, to test tubes 1 and 2. Mix the Junket with the milk, using a stirring rod.

❑ **3.** **OBSERVE:** Half fill the 250-mL beaker with water and place it on the heat source. Place test tubes 1 and 3 into the beaker of water. Warm the test tubes in the heated water. Do not boil the water. ⚠ CAUTION: **Hold each test tube with a test-tube clamp when placing it into or taking it out of the water. Do not point the test tubes toward yourself or anyone else.** Does the liquid in either test tube coagulate, or thicken? Write your observations in Table 1. Remove the test tubes from the beaker and place them in the test-tube rack. Turn off the heat source.

❑ **4.** **OBSERVE:** Place test tube 2 in the beaker of water and heat the test tube to boiling. ⚠ CAUTION: **Observe all safety rules when boiling a liquid.** Does the liquid coagulate? Write your observation in Table 1.

❑ **5.** Set up the equipment for filtering the liquids, as shown in Figure 1.

❑ **6.** Filter the contents of test tube 1 by pouring it through the funnel and filter paper into the clean test tube 4. Use a spatula to remove the solid material from the filter paper and place it in the 100-mL beaker with a little water.

❑ **7.** **OBSERVE:** Add a few drops of Biuret solution to the mixture in the beaker. Stir. Do you see a color change? Biuret solution turns purple in the presence of protein. Record your observations in Table 1.

❑ **8.** **OBSERVE:** Add a few drops of Biuret solution to test tube 4 (the liquid that you filtered from test tube 1). Stir the mixture. Record your observations.

❑ **9.** Wash the dropper. Use it to put a small amount of apple juice on a watch glass. Then, wash the dropper again. Use the dropper to add a few drops of Biuret solution to the apple juice. Stir. Record your observations.

Materials
safety goggles
lab apron
4 test tubes
milk
wax pencil
test-tube rack
tablespoon
powdered Junket
glass stirring rod
250-mL beaker
water
test-tube clamp
heat source
funnel
filter paper
spatula
100-mL beaker
Biuret solution
dropper
apple juice
watch glass

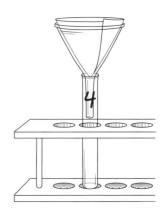

▲ **Figure 1** Filtering setup

OBSERVATIONS

Table 1: Action of Rennin			
Container	**Contents**	**Action**	**Observations**
Test tube 1	milk, rennin	warm	
Test tube 2	milk, rennin	boiling	
Test tube 3	milk	warm	
Beaker	solid material from test tube 1, water	add Biuret solution	
Test tube 4	filtered liquid from test tube 1	add Biuret solution	
Watch glass	apple juice	add Biuret solution	

1. **IDENTIFY:** Biuret solution turns violet in the presence of protein. In which steps of the procedure did you find protein?

   _____

2. **IDENTIFY:** Does the apple juice contain protein? How do you know?

   _____

CONCLUSIONS

3. **INFER:** What caused the milk in test tube 1 to coagulate? _____

4. **INFER:** Why do you think the test tubes were warmed? _____

   _____

5. **ANALYZE:** How do you know that just warming milk does not cause it to coagulate?

   _____

   _____

6. **DESCRIBE:** Describe the action of rennin on milk. On what nutrient does rennin act?

   _____

   _____

Name _____ Class _____ Date _____

How does the heart move blood through the body?

BACKGROUND: The heart constantly pumps blood through the body. Each time the heart beats, blood moves into and through the arteries in spurts, or pulses. This pulse rate is the same as a heartbeat. You cannot see your own heart pumping blood. You can, however, observe the heartbeat of a tiny water animal called a daphnia.

PURPOSE: In this activity, you will observe the beating heart of a daphnia as it pumps blood and compare it to your own heartbeat.

Materials
daphnia
water
dropper
microscope slide with well
coverslip
microscope
clock or watch with second hand

PROCEDURE

Part A: Measuring the Rate of a Daphnia's Heartbeat

☐ 1. Use a dropper to place a daphnia and a drop of water in the well of a microscope slide, as shown in Figure 1. Place a coverslip on the slide.

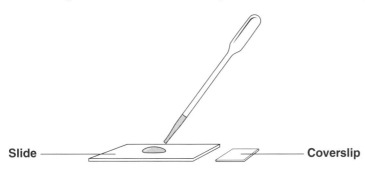

Slide ———————————— Coverslip

▲ **Figure 1** Daphnia on a microscope slide

☐ 2. **OBSERVE:** Look at the daphnia under the microscope, using the low-power objective. To observe the different parts of the daphnia, you will have to rotate the diaphragm. This will cut down on the amount of light.

☐ 3. **OBSERVE:** Find the heart of the daphnia. It looks like a small, almost-clear ball moving rapidly back and forth. Figure 2 shows the placement of the heart at the top of the daphnia, behind its eyes. Do not mistake the daphnia's quick movements for the heartbeat. The heart beats much faster than the daphnia moves. If the movement you are looking at starts and stops, it is not the heartbeat.

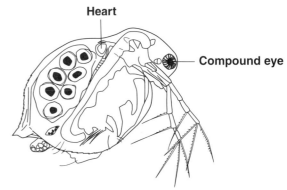

▲ **Figure 2** Parts of a daphnia

❏ 4. **MEASURE:** Have your lab partner look at a watch with a second hand while you are looking through the microscope at the daphnia's heart. Count the number of times the daphnia's heart beats in 15 seconds. Your lab partner should tell you when to start counting and when the 15 seconds have passed. Record the number of heartbeats you counted in Table 1.

❏ 5. **CALCULATE:** Multiply the number of beats you counted in 15 seconds by 4 to find the number of heartbeats in 1 min. Record this number in Table 1.

Number of beats in 1 min = number of beats in 15 sec × 4

❏ 6. Repeat Steps 4 and 5 two more times. Record your measurements and calculations in Table 1.

❏ 7. Add the beats per minute for each trial. Divide this number by 3 to find the average number of heartbeats per min. Record this average in Table 1.

Total number of beats = beats in trial 1 + beats in trial 2 + beats in trial 3

Average number of heartbeats per min = total number of beats ÷ 3

❏ 8. Follow your teacher's instructions for cleaning up your work area. Wash your hands.

Table 1: Daphnia Heartbeat Rate		
Trial	Number of Beats in 15 Sec	Number of Beats in 1 Min
1		
2		
3		
		Average:

LABORATORY CHALLENGE FOR LESSON 15-3 *(continued)*

Part B: Measuring the Rate of Your Heartbeat

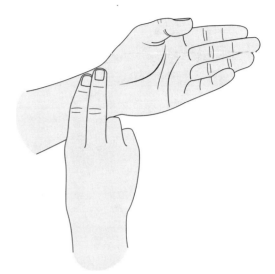

▲ **Figure 3** Finding a pulse

❏ 1. **OBSERVE:** Find your own pulse by placing your middle and index fingers of one hand on the inside wrist of the other hand, as shown in Figure 3. Move your fingers around slowly on your wrist until you can feel a strong throb.

❏ 2. **MEASURE:** Remain still for 2 min. This will allow you to measure your pulse rate after you have been resting. Then, count the number of pulses that you feel in 15 sec. Your lab partner can look at a watch and tell you when to start and stop counting. Write the number of beats in Table 2.

❏ 3. **CALCULATE:** Multiply the number of beats you counted in 15 seconds by 4 to find the number of heartbeats in 1 min, just as you did when measuring the daphnia's heartbeat rate. Record this number in Table 2.

❏ 4. **CALCULATE:** Take your pulse two more times. Each time, multiply the number by 4 to determine the number of beats per min. Record your results in Table 2.

❏ 5. **CALCULATE:** Find the average rate for your three trials by adding the results for each trial and dividing by 3, just as you did when measuring the daphnia's heartbeat rate. Record your results in Table 2.

	Table 2: Human Heartbeat Rate	
Trial	Number of Beats in 15 Sec	Number of Beats in 1 Min
1		
2		
3		
		Average:

OBSERVATIONS

1. **IDENTIFY:** Does the heartbeat of the daphnia seem to speed up and slow down, or does it seem to maintain a constant rate?

   _____

2. **OBSERVE:** Were you able to see the blood of the daphnia? Explain why or why not.

   _____

   _____

3. **IDENTIFY:** What is the daphnia's average number of heartbeats per min?

   _____

4. **IDENTIFY:** What is your average pulse rate?

   _____

CONCLUSIONS

5. **INFER:** Why was it useful to take three measurements for the daphnia's heartbeat rate and for your pulse rate?

   _____

   _____

6. **DESCRIBE:** How does blood move through your arteries?

   _____

   _____

7. **INFER:** How is your pulse rate related to your heartbeat rate?

   _____

   _____

8. **COMPARE:** How does your pulse rate compare with that of a daphnia?

   _____

LABORATORY CHALLENGE FOR LESSON 16-4

How is air exchanged in the lungs?

BACKGROUND: The air that you breathe contains oxygen. When you inhale, oxygen enters your body through the lungs. Red blood cells carry the oxygen from your lungs to all cells of your body. Blood cells also carry waste materials, such as water and carbon dioxide, from your body's cells back to your lungs. Waste materials leave your body through your lungs when you exhale.

PURPOSE: In this activity, you will investigate how air is exchanged in the lungs. You will also investigate the effect of exercise on your breathing rate.

PROCEDURE

Part A: Investigating Sponge and Lung Tissue

❑ 1. Put on a lab apron.

❑ 2. **OBSERVE:** Break off a piece of the sponge. Examine its surface and the inside. What does the sponge look like?
Write your observation in Table 1 on page 78.

❑ 3. **OBSERVE:** Place the sponge in a beaker of water, as shown in Figure 1. What feature of the sponge's structure helps it float? Write your observations in Table 1.

❑ 4. **OBSERVE:** Obtain a prepared slide of lung tissue. Look at the slide under a microscope, using the low-power objective.

❑ 5. **MODEL:** Draw a sketch of the lung tissue in the space labeled Diagram 1.

❑ 6. **COMPARE:** Compare the appearance of the lung tissue with the sponge. Write your observations in Table 1.

Materials
safety goggles
lab apron
sponge
250-mL beaker
water
prepared slide of lung tissue
microscope
mirror
test tube
limewater
drinking straw
clock or watch with second hand

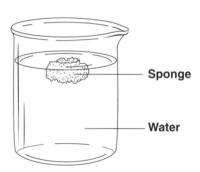

▲ **Figure 1** Place the sponge in the beaker.

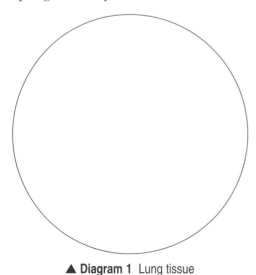

▲ **Diagram 1** Lung tissue

Table 1: Observing Sponge and Lung Tissue	
Question	**Observations**
What does a sponge look like?	
What helps the sponge float?	
How does the lung tissue look like a sponge?	

Part B: Investigating Your Breath

☐ 1. **OBSERVE:** Hold a small mirror in front of your mouth and breathe out on it with your mouth wide open. What forms on the mirror? Write your observation in Table 2.

☐ 2. Put on safety goggles.

☐ 3. Limewater turns cloudy in the presence of carbon dioxide. Fill a test tube about one-quarter full with limewater. Use a straw to blow into the limewater, as shown in Figure 2. ⚠ **CAUTION: Do not taste or inhale the limewater.** Notice what happens to the limewater. Write your observation in Table 2.

Part C: Investigating Your Breathing Rate

☐ 1. **OBSERVE:** Check your breathing rate while you are sitting or standing still. Using a clock or watch with a second hand, count the number of times you inhale in 1 min. Write your results in Table 2.

☐ 2. **OBSERVE:** Jump up and down 20 times. Check your breathing rate again. Record your results in Table 2.

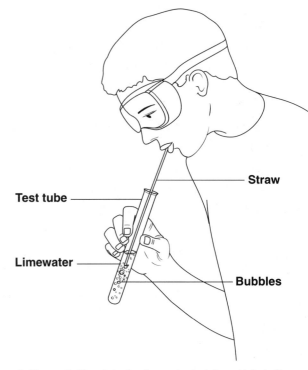

Test tube

Straw

Limewater

Bubbles

▲ **Figure 2** Blow into the limewater but do not inhale it.

LABORATORY CHALLENGE FOR LESSON 16-4 *(continued)*

OBSERVATIONS

Table 2: Analyzing Breath	
Action	**Observations**
Breathe on mirror	
Blow into limewater	
Count number of breaths per min while still	
Count number of breaths per min after jumping	

1. **INFER:** When you breathed on the mirror, where did the water droplets come from?

_____

2. **OBSERVE:** What happened to your breathing rate after you jumped up and down?

_____

CONCLUSIONS

3. **COMPARE:** How is air entering and leaving the lungs like water entering and leaving the sponge?

_____

_____

4. **MODEL:** In what way does lung tissue look like a sponge?

_____

_____

5. ANALYZE: What did your test with limewater show about breath?

_____

_____

6. INFER: The gas present in your exhaled breath is a byproduct of what
cell process?

_____

_____

CRITICAL THINKING

7. HYPOTHESIZE: Why do you breathe harder when you are running than when you
are walking?

_____

_____

LABORATORY CHALLENGE FOR LESSON 17-3

How can an infection be spread?

BACKGROUND: Many diseases are caused by microorganisms. These diseases are called infectious diseases. Some microorganisms that cause infectious diseases are spread through the air. Some are spread through water or food. Some infectious diseases are spread by contact with an infected person.

PURPOSE: In this activity, you will transfer microorganisms and observe their effects. The microorganisms that you use will not be true causes of disease. They will be bacteria of decay that you can use to model how an infectious disease may spread.

Materials
safety goggles
lab apron
gloves
3 fresh apples
rotten apple
marking pen
3 plastic knives
3 small paper plates
tincture of iodine
dropper

PROCEDURE

❏ 1. Put on safety goggles, a lab apron, and gloves.

❏ 2. Using the marking pen, label the three fresh apples *A*, *B*, and *C*.

❏ 3. Pick up one of the clean knives, touching only the knife handle. Stick the point of the knife into apple *A,* as shown in Figure 1. ⚠ **CAUTION: Be careful when handling the knife.** Make a cut with the serrated part of the knife. Then, stick the knife into the cut. Remove the knife. Set the apple on a clean paper plate. Discard the knife.

❏ 4. Stick the point of a second clean plastic knife into the decayed part of the rotten apple. Withdraw the knife and stick the point into apple B. Put apple B on a second clean paper plate and set it aside. Discard the knife.

❏ 5. Push the point of the third clean knife into the decayed part of the rotten apple, as you did in Step 4. Withdraw the knife and stick the knife's point into apple C. Withdraw the knife.

❏ 6. Use the dropper to place two or three drops of iodine over the cut made by the knife in apple C, as shown in Figure 2. Be careful with the iodine. It stains skin and clothing. Use the knife to push the iodine into the hole so that it fills the hole. Set this apple on the third clean paper plate.

❏ 7. **OBSERVE:** Leave the three fresh apples exposed to the air at room temperature. Examine them each day for 3 days. Look for changes in the apples. Write your observations in Table 1.

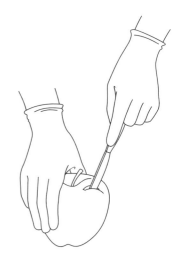

▲ **Figure 1** Carefully stick the plastic knife into apple A.

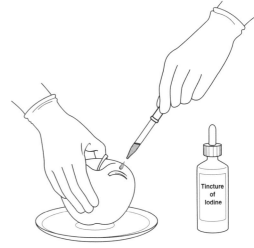

▲ **Figure 2** Place iodine into the cut in apple C.

OBSERVATIONS

Table 1: Observing the Spread of Bacteria				
		Observations		
Apple	Pierced With:	Day 1	Day 2	Day 3
A	clean knife			
B	knife stuck into rotten apple			
C	knife stuck into rotten apple; hole covered with iodine			

CONCLUSIONS

1. **IDENTIFY:** Which apple in this experiment was the control? _____

2. **IDENTIFY:** How were bacteria spread to apples B and C? _____

_____

_____

3. **RELATE:** In what similar way might bacteria enter a human?

_____

_____

4. **INFER:** Why were the results different with apple C than with apple B?

_____

_____

5. **INFER:** What method of disease prevention does this experiment illustrate?

_____

_____

LABORATORY CHALLENGE FOR LESSON 18-4

How do the senses of taste and smell work together?

BACKGROUND: Your tongue alone does not determine the taste of foods you eat. In fact, your tongue can be fooled. You need both your senses of taste and smell to identify many of the foods you eat.

PURPOSE: In this activity, you will work with a partner to find out how the nose and tongue work together to identify different flavors.

PROCEDURE

- ❑ **1.** Put on safety goggles, a lab apron, and disposable gloves.
- ❑ **2.** Use a plastic knife to peel an apple, a potato, and an onion. ⚠ **CAUTION: Be very careful when using sharp objects.**
- ❑ **3.** Cut each peeled food into small cubes, all about the same size. Put the cubes of each type of food on a separate paper plate. Mark a folded index card with the name of each food, as shown in Figure 1.

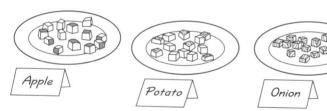

▲ **Figure 1** Put each kind of food on a separate plate.

- ❑ **4.** Place a teaspoonful of salt onto a paper plate. Place a teaspoonful of sugar onto another paper plate. On two folded index cards, write *Salt* and *Sugar* and place them in front of each plate.
- ❑ **5.** Fill a paper cup with water. Put the cup nearby.
- ❑ **6.** Have your partner close his or her eyes or wear a blindfold.
- ❑ **7.** **IDENTIFY:** Pick up one of the food cubes with a toothpick and feed it to your partner, as shown in Figure 2. He or she should taste the food, but does not have to swallow it. The food can be spit out onto a napkin or paper towel. Ask your partner to tell you what the food is. If your partner guesses correctly, put a check mark in the first box under that food in Table 1 on page 84. If your partner guesses wrong, put an X in the box.

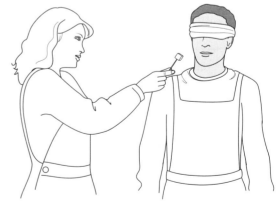

▲ **Figure 2** Use a toothpick to feed your partner a food cube.

Materials

safety goggles
lab apron
disposable gloves
plastic knife
raw apple
raw potato
raw onion
5 paper plates
5 index cards
marking pen
teaspoon
salt
sugar
2 paper cups
water
napkins or paper towels
box of toothpicks
blindfold (optional)

☐ **8. IDENTIFY:** Have your partner rinse his or her mouth with water, keeping eyes closed or the blindfold on. Then, repeat Step 7 with another food cube. It can be the same food or a different one. Be sure to use a clean toothpick for each trial.

☐ **9. IDENTIFY:** Repeat Step 7 until your partner has tasted every food twice. You can choose the different food cubes in any order.

☐ **10.** Have your partner continue to keep eyes closed or a blindfold on. This time, however, ask your partner to hold his or her nose closed with the thumb and index finger.

☐ **11. IDENTIFY:** Repeat the six taste tests in a different order. Remember to have your partner rinse with water after each test. Record the results of the tests in Table 2 on page 85.

☐ **12. IDENTIFY:** Feed your partner one food while holding a different food under his or her nose. Again, perform the six food tests in any order. For each test, hold a different food under your partner's nose. Record the results in Table 3.

☐ **13.** Prepare six pieces of potato. Leave two of the pieces plain. Lightly coat two pieces by touching them to the salt. Lightly coat two pieces by touching them to the sugar.

☐ **14. IDENTIFY:** Use a toothpick to feed one of the six pieces to your partner, Your partner should hold his or her nose closed again and try to identify the piece as plain, salty, or sweet. Record a correct response with a check mark or an incorrect response with an X in Table 4.

☐ **15. IDENTIFY:** Repeat Step 14 for each of the remaining five pieces of potato. Choose the pieces in any order. Have your partner rinse with water after each test. Record the results in Table 4.

☐ **16. IDENTIFY:** Change places with your partner. Prepare a new cup of water and have new toothpicks available. Have your partner give you the same tests. Record the results in Tables 1, 2, 3, and 4.

OBSERVATIONS

Table 1: Food Identification: Taste and Smell		Apple	Potato	Onion
Lab Partner 1	Trial 1			
	Trial 2			
Lab Partner 2	Trial 1			
	Trial 2			

LABORATORY CHALLENGE FOR LESSON 18-4 *(continued)*

Table 2: Food Identification: Taste Only		Apple	Potato	Onion
Lab Partner 1	Trial 1			
	Trial 2			
Lab Partner 2	Trial 1			
	Trial 2			

Table 3: Food Identification: Taste With Different Smell		Apple	Potato	Onion
Lab Partner 1	Trial 1			
	Trial 2			
Lab Partner 2	Trial 1			
	Trial 2			

Table 4: Food Identification: Food With Sugar or Salt		Plain Potato	Salty Potato	Sugary Potato
Lab Partner 1	Trial 1			
	Trial 2			
Lab Partner 2	Trial 1			
	Trial 2			

CONCLUSIONS

1. **IDENTIFY:** Were you and your partner able to identify foods better by taste and smell, by taste alone, or by taste with different smell?

_____

_____

_____

2. **COMPARE:** How did your results compare with your partner's results?

_____

_____

_____

3. **ANALYZE:** Was there anything other than taste and smell that helped you in distinguishing the food? Explain.

_____

_____

_____

4. **ANALYZE:** Were you always able to distinguish between salty and sweet tastes without using your sense of smell?

_____

_____

5. **ANALYZE:** Can taste alone always tell you what you are eating? Explain.

_____

6. **INFER:** How do you think your nose helps your brain identify foods?

_____

_____

_____

_____

LABORATORY CHALLENGE FOR LESSON 18-5

How does the eye work?

BACKGROUND: When light enters your eye, it passes through the cornea and then through the lens. The lens then directs light to the area at the back of your eye, called the retina, where the image forms. You see the image when your optic nerve, which is behind the retina, sends impulses to your brain.

PURPOSE: In this activity, you and a partner will observe how the eye responds to changes in light. You will also observe how the blind spot affects vision and learn what is meant by persistence of vision.

Materials

penlight

index card

marking pen

photocopy of bird and cage on page 89

scissors

glue

piece of heavy white paper or oak tag

pencil

PROCEDURE

Part A: Response of Eyes to Changes in Light

❏ 1. **OBSERVE:** Look at the illustrations of the eye in Figure 1. Notice the location of the iris. The iris is the colored part of the eye. The pupil, which looks like a black circle in the middle of the iris, is an opening in the iris.

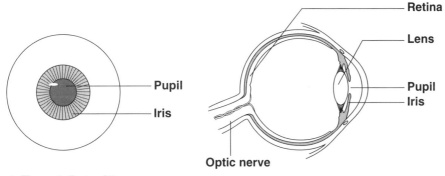

▲ **Figure 1** Parts of the eye

❏ 2. **OBSERVE:** Look at your partner's eyes. Locate the iris and the pupil of each eye. Notice the size of the pupils.

❏ 3. **OBSERVE:** Have your partner close his or her eyes for about 1 min. Observe what happens to the size of the pupils as your partner's eyes open. Write your observations in Table 1 on page 89.

❏ 4. Shine the beam of a penlight for a few seconds into one of your partner's eyes, as shown in Figure 2. The light should be about 30 cm away from the eye. What happens to the pupil of the eye? What about the pupil of the other eye? Write your observations in Table 1.

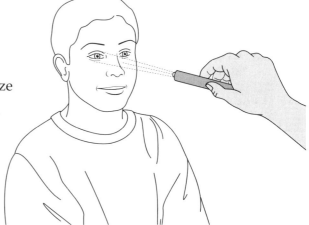

▲ **Figure 2** Shine the penlight into your partner's eye.

Part B: The Blind Spot

❏ **1. IDENTIFY:** Look again at the diagram of the eye in Figure 1. Notice where the optic nerve meets the retina. This is called the blind spot. Your eye is unable to form an image from light that hits this spot. In the next few steps of this activity, you will prove that both of your eyes have blind spots.

❏ **2.** Use a marking pen to draw an *X* on the left side and an *O* on the right side of an index card, as shown in Figure 3.

❏ **3.** Cover your left eye. Hold the index card straight out in front of you at arm's length, as shown in Figure 4. The side of the card with the *X* and *O* should be facing you. Focus your right eye on the *X* at the left side of the card. You will be able to see the *O* on the right side without looking at it directly.

▲ **Figure 3** Draw an X and an O on an index card.

▲ **Figure 4** Hold an index card and cover your left eye.

❏ **4. OBSERVE:** Slowly move the card toward you, but keep focusing on the *X* on the left side. What happens to the *O*? Continue slowly moving the card closer to your eye. Does this cause any other change in the *O*? Repeat this test several times, slowly moving the card back and forth, making careful observations. Repeat the test with your right eye closed while you look at the *O* with your left eye. Record your observations in Table 1.

Part C: Persistence of Vision

❏ **1.** Obtain a photocopy of Figure 6 on page 89. Do not cut out the figures from your lab manual.

❏ **2.** Use glue to attach the photocopy to heavy white paper to make it stiff. Cut out the bird and the cage separately. ⚠ **CAUTION: Be careful when using scissors.** Then, glue the picture of the bird and the picture of the cage together back-to-back on a pencil, as shown in Figure 7. Be sure that the pictures are on the outside.

LABORATORY CHALLENGE FOR LESSON 18-5 *(continued)*

▲ **Figure 6** Cut out a photocopy of the bird and cage.

▲ **Figure 7** Glue the bird and cage back-to-back on a pencil.

☐ 3. **OBSERVE:** When an image is formed on the retina, it remains there for a short time, even after the eye is no longer looking at the object. This is called persistence of vision. Hold the pencil between the palms of your hands and move your palms back and forth. This action causes the bird and cage to spin first one way and then the other. Observe what happens to the image of the bird as you spin quickly. Observe what happens if you spin very slowly. Write your observations in Table 1.

OBSERVATIONS

Table 1: How the Eye Works	
Action	**Observations**
Closing eyes for 1 min, then opening them	
Penlight shining in eye	
Moving the index card with X and O at different distances from eyes	
Spinning the bird-and-cage cards	

CONCLUSIONS

1. **DESCRIBE:** How did your partner's eyes react to increased and decreased light?

_____

_____

2. **DESCRIBE:** Do eyes seem to react slowly or quickly to changes in the brightness of light?

_____

3. **INFER:** When do you think the pupil of the eye would be open the widest?

_____

4. **INFER:** How are you able to tell that each of your eyes has a blind spot?

_____

_____

5. **DESCRIBE:** What causes the blind spot?

_____

_____

6. **RELATE:** Explain why the image of the bird appears in the cage when the bird-and-cage is spun quickly but not when it is spun slowly.

_____

_____

_____

Name _____ Class _____ Date _____

How does the rate of human development change with age?

> **Materials**
>
> cloth tape measure
> pens (2 different colors)
> graph paper

BACKGROUND: Many changes occur in the human body from birth through age 20, but the changes do not occur at a constant rate. A baby experiences rapid increases in height, weight, and head size during the first six months after birth. Growth usually ends when a person is about 20 years old.

PURPOSE: In this activity, you will investigate human development by creating and comparing growth charts for height and head circumference.

PROCEDURE

☐ 1. **GRAPH:** Table 1 shows the average height for girls and boys from birth through age 20. On a sheet of graph paper, set up a graph so that Age (years) is on the horizontal axis and Height (cm) is on the vertical axis. Use one color pen to plot the heights for girls on the graph. Make a line graph by connecting the points with a line. Use the other color pen to plot the heights for boys on the same graph. Connect the points.

☐ 2. **MEASURE:** Stand with your back to a wall. Have your lab partner use a tape measure to measure your height in centimeters. Mark your height on the graph with an X.

Table 1: Average Height								
Age (years)	Girls (cm)	Boys (cm)	Age (years)	Girls (cm)	Boys (cm)	Age (years)	Girls (cm)	Boys (cm)
0	49	50	7	122	122	14	160	164
1	74	76	8	128	128	15	162	170
2	86	87	9	133	133	16	162	173
3	95	96	10	138	139	17	163	175
4	101	102	11	144	143	18	163	176
5	108	109	12	151	149	19	163	177
6	115	115	13	157	156	20	163	177

Table 2: Average Head Circumferences												
Age (mo.)	0	3	6	9	12	15	18	21	24	27	30	33	36
Girls (cm)	34.8	40.0	42.4	43.9	45.0	45.9	46.6	47.0	47.4	47.8	48.2	48.4	48.6
Boys (cm)	35.8	41.3	43.6	45.2	46.4	47.2	47.8	48.2	48.7	49.0	49.3	49.5	49.6

❏ 3. **GRAPH:** Table 2 shows the average head circumferences for girls and boys from birth through 36 months. Use a separate sheet of graph paper to create a line graph for this information. Remember to use different colors on the graph for the two sets of data. Also remember to label the horizontal and vertical axes.

❏ 4. **MEASURE:** Use the tape measure to find the circumference of your head. Write the measurement on the line below. You will use this information to answer question 7. _____

OBSERVATIONS

1. **IDENTIFY:** At approximately what age do girls reach their maximum height? _____

2. **IDENTIFY:** At approximately what age do boys reach their maximum height? _____

3. **IDENTIFY:** During what years do girls have an average height greater then boys? _____

4. **IDENTIFY:** Are there any ages when girls have a greater average head circumference than boys? _____

CONCLUSIONS

5. **PREDICT:** Based on the data in Table 2, would you expect the head circumference of a person to be much greater or slightly greater at age 20 than it was at age 3? Explain.

_____

_____

_____

6. **ANALYZE:** If you knew how tall a child was at age 2, would it be possible to tell what the child's height would be at age 20? Why or why not?

_____

_____

7. **ANALYZE:** When girls and boys are 3 years old, their head circumferences are about half their height. If this were true for you now, what would your head circumference be? How does this compare to your actual head circumference?

_____

_____

_____